An Illustrated History of the Church

Created and Produced by Jaca Book

The First Christians
From the beginnings to A.D. 180

The Church Established
A.D. 180—381

The End of the Ancient World
A.D. 381—600

The Formation of Christian Europe
A.D. 600—900

The Middle Ages
A.D. 900—1300

**The Breakdown
of Medieval Christendom**
A.D. 1300—1500

Protestant and Catholic Reform
A.D. 1500—1700

The Church in Revolutionary Times
A.D. 1700—1850

The Church and the Modern Nations
A.D. 1850—1945

The Church Today
A.D. 1945 and after

An outline by chapter and a suggested reading list
can be found on the last two pages of this volume.

The First Christians

An Illustrated History of the Church

From the Beginnings to A.D. 180

Translated and adapted by John Drury
Illustrated by Antonio Molino

Winston Press   430 Oak Grove   Minneapolis, Minnesota 55403

Published in Italy under the title
I primi Cristiani: La chiesa e la sua storia
Copyright © 1979 Jaca Book Edizioni

**Licensed publisher and distributor
of the English-language edition:**

Winston Press, Inc.
430 Oak Grove
Minneapolis, Minnesota 55403
United States of America

Agents:
Canada—
  LeDroit/Novalis-Select
  135 Nelson St.
  Ottawa, Ontario
  Canada   KIN   7R4

Australia, New Zealand, New Guinea, Fiji Islands—
  Dove Communications, Pty. Ltd.
  203 Darling Road
  East Malvern, Victoria   3145
  Australia

United Kingdom, Ireland, and South Africa—
  Fowler-Wright Books, Ltd.
  Burgess St.
  Leominster, Herefordshire
  England

Acknowledgments
Scripture texts used in chapters 1 through 31 are taken from the *New American Bible*, copyright © 1970 by the Confraternity of Christian Doctrine, Washington, D.C. Used by permission of the copyright owner. All rights reserved.

The Scripture quotations in chapters 32 through 36 are from the *Revised Standard Version Common Bible*, copyright © 1973 by the Division of Christian Education of the National Council of the Churches of Christ in the U.S.A. Used by permission.

Created and produced by Jaca Book, Milan
Color selection: Carlo Scotti, Milan
Printing: Grafiche Lithos, Carugate, Milan
Binding: LEM Opera, Milan

Winston Staff: Mark Brokering, Florence Flugaur—editorial
              Chris Larson, Keith McCormick—design
Special Editorial Assistance: Joan Mitchell, CSJ

Copyright © 1980, English-language edition,
Jaca Book, Milan, Italy. All rights reserved.
Printed in Italy.

Library of Congress Catalog Card Number: 79-67830
ISBN: 0-03-056823-4
5 4 3 2 1

An Illustrated History of the Church

The First Christians

Introduction

This ten-volume history of the Church presents in a broad sweep the people, events, and ideas that have made up the continuous life of the Christian community through nearly two thousand years. The greatest impact of these volumes for young people lies in the simple fact that the Church has a history.

In our years of growing out of childhood and into adolescence, we become capable of developing a sense of history—a sense we refine throughout life. This sense of history is necessary because we human beings live in time. Through the interpretation of past events, people, and their significance, we claim the past, live the present, and shape the future. For this reason, families remember their ancestors, whose lives encourage, whose mistakes enlighten, whose values inspire, whose accomplishments give hope. For this reason, cultures and nations remember their founders, their leaders, their givers of meaning. And for this reason, this history of the Church offers young Christians an account of their faith ancestry as an inheritance for their own becoming.

The Christian community spans centuries, leaps national boundaries, and expresses itself in diverse cultures and lives today. Its history introduces us to cultural, racial, ethnic, and national groups unlike our own, yet sharing—as the Letter to the Ephesians says—one Spirit, one hope, one Lord, one faith, one Baptism, one God and Father of all. In these volumes, the reader will find the expanse and shape of the Church's history. Young people will find this history in the short chapters that focus on real people, important conflicts, and decisive councils—with illustrations that invite them to see other times, cultures, and lands.

This volume covers the first two centuries of the Church's history—from its beginnings until A.D. 180. Its fifty-nine chapters tell of Jesus' life, the apostles' proclamation of his death and resurrection, the formation of the New Testament, the Church's separation from Judaism, and the Church's organization and problems.

On our bookshelves in classrooms, libraries, and homes, these volumes hold for us a future to be shaped and a past to be claimed.

Joan Mitchell, CSJ

1. To understand the history of the Church, we must look at the history of the people among whom the Church began: the people of Israel. Over a thousand years before the Church began, God chose the people of Israel as his own. He led them out of Egypt, made a covenant with them, and brought them to the land he had promised.

Among all the peoples of the world, God showed his love to the people of Israel in a special way. The early Israelites were called *Hebrews*, which means wanderers or nomads. Around 1500 B.C., some Hebrew tribes became slaves in Egypt. Then in the 1200s B.C., God raised up a great man named Moses. God told his name to Moses—*Yahweh*, which means *I am who am*—and sent him to free the Hebrew slaves. Moses persuaded the Israelites to flee Egypt. They wandered in the desert for forty years before reaching the land God had promised them—the land of Canaan.

At Mount Sinai in the desert, Yahweh made an agreement of mutual loyalty with the Hebrews. God promised to be with them always, to love and help them. He asked the people in return to recognize him alone as God. This agreement or covenant made clear how the people were to show that they believed in Yahweh. The terms of this covenant

are the laws we call the ten commandments.

Yahweh kept his covenant with the Hebrews. In the desert, they ate quail and manna and drank water, the blessings of their creator. Yahweh stayed with them as they conquered the promised land and became a nation under their greatest king—David.

The people already living in this land worshiped many gods. They fashioned images and statues of their gods in gold, silver, bronze, and stone. But the God of the Israelites was the living God, who loved, helped, and forgave his people. No one could make an image of him. Yahweh could not be confined to one place or worshiped in the form of an image.

For over four hundred years after King David (1000 B.C.), the people of Israel existed as a nation. Many times during these years, they forgot their covenant with Yahweh by cheating, neglecting the poor, or even worshiping the gods of their neighbors. Yahweh raised up prophets to call the people to remember the covenant. When even Israel's kings worshiped other gods, the prophets spoke sharply. One of them named Isaiah dreamed of a king greater than David who would come and save his people. This savior came to be called the Messiah or, in Greek, the Christ, which means the anointed one.

Despite their forgetfulness of Yahweh and the covenant, the Israelites managed to keep one conviction while living in the midst of other peoples. This was the conviction that the one and only God guided them at all times. Thus their religion was different from those religions that professed belief in many gods. Moreover, thanks to the voices of the prophets, the people never forgot that Yahweh brought them out of Egypt, made a covenant with them, and promised a king greater than David to raise them above the kingdoms of this earth.

2. At the time of Jesus' birth, the Israelite people lived under Roman rule. Their law and their worship kept them together as a people. They vividly recalled God's promise to send a great king, the Messiah, to save and liberate them.

For over five hundred years before the birth of Jesus, other nations had ruled Israel—first the Assyrians, then the Babylonians, the Persians, the Greeks, and finally the Romans. At the time of Jesus' birth, the Romans had conquered most of the then known world and ruled many peoples, including the Jews.

In every province of the empire, the Roman emperor appointed a governor to ensure order and loyalty. Roman soldiers kept order in every city of Galilee, Samaria, and Judea—the areas where Jesus lived and taught. In every city, too, government officials and agents collected taxes owed to the Roman emperor.

The Jewish people were not content. They felt humiliated and oppressed under foreign rule. But their own law kept them together as a people. It told them how to keep the Sabbath, how to worship, who to marry, what to eat. The law helped the Israelites remember that they were the people who believed in the one, true God, Yahweh,

through all the time of foreign rule. When they went to Jerusalem to worship at the temple on holy days, they knew they were one as a people. They climbed the road to Jerusalem singing songs of Yahweh. They brought offerings to the temple and worshiped together. Many hoped that God would send their Savior, the Messiah, to free them from the Romans.

Into this world, Jesus was born of a woman named Mary, who lived in Nazareth in Galilee. Nazareth was not a place of major importance. It was a small town in the hill country of Galilee. On market days, its hard-working inhabitants crowded the streets to see the wares being sold. None of them could have foreseen that the one so anxiously awaited by the Jewish people would come from this town. None of them, meeting Mary on the street or at the spring where they drew water, could have guessed that this simple young lady of the town would be chosen by God to be the mother of the world's Messiah.

3. God kept his promise of a Savior—a Savior whose resurrection from the dead would be the beginning of the Christian Church. God sent an angel to ask Mary if she would agree to become the mother of this Messiah, who would be the Son of God. Mary said yes to God. Thus the most important turning point in the story of God's friendship with human beings got under way in secret.

The Christian Church began on the first Easter, when the risen Jesus sent the Holy Spirit upon his followers, giving them strength and courage to tell the whole world about his new life. For the rest of their lives, these witnesses of Jesus' resurrection proclaimed the good news of Jesus' life, death, and resurrection. After forty years, Mark collected many of the proclamations, stories, sayings, and parables they preached about Jesus. These were written into one continuous story—the first Gospel. Matthew's and Luke's Gospels were written later, using Mark's Gospel and other traditions. Near the end of the first century, John's Gospel was written. Each of these books, from beginning to end, proclaims that Jesus' followers believed in his resurrection and that they realized he had been the Son of God all his life.

The story in Luke's Gospel of God's invitation to Mary to become the mother of Jesus shows that she said yes to becoming the mother of the Messiah. When Mary was

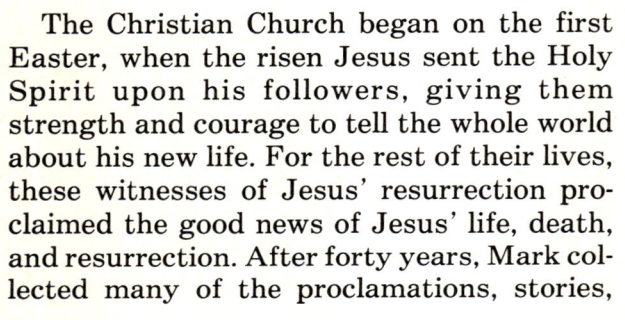

about fifteen years old and planning to marry a young man named Joseph, an angel sent by God appeared to her, saying: "Rejoice, O highly favored daughter! The Lord is with you!" Mary was troubled by these words. She wondered what they meant. But the angel reassured her: "Do not fear, Mary. You have found favor with God. You shall conceive and bear a son and give him the name Jesus. Great will be his dignity and he will be called Son of the Most High. The Lord God will give him the throne of David his father" (Luke 1:28-32).

Mary asked how this could be since she was not yet married to Joseph. The angel replied that this baby would not be the son of the young man she would marry. "The Holy Spirit will come upon you and the power of the Most High will overshadow you; hence, the holy offspring to be born will be called Son of God.... nothing is impossible with God" (Luke 1:35-37). Mary knew that the angel was waiting for her to say yes, so that the miracle could take place. Her response shows that she was the first and most important believer in Jesus. She said, "I am the servant of the Lord. Let it be done to me as you say" (Luke 1:38).

4. Matthew's story of the birth of Jesus shows that Jesus was the Son of David whom God promised to send as the Messiah. Joseph, a descendant of the house of David, agreed to take care of Mary and the baby she had conceived by the Holy Spirit. Mary and Joseph journeyed to Bethlehem, the city of David, where Jesus would be born.

Matthew wrote his Gospel for Jewish Christians, so he made connections between Jesus and the promised Messiah, who was expected to come from the house of David. Matthew began his story of Jesus by focusing on Joseph, Jesus' foster father, who belonged to the house or line of David.

Joseph was engaged, but not married, to Mary when he found out that she was expecting a baby. Since the child did not belong to him, he considered not going through with the marriage. But Joseph, an upright man, did not want to subject Mary to the punishment of the law for unfaithfulness, so he decided to end the engagement secretly. In this, he imitated the kindness of God rather than imposing the severity of human laws.

Then Joseph had a dream. In the dream, an angel told him that he should not fear taking Mary for his wife, because she had conceived the child by the Holy Spirit. The angel told Joseph to name the child Jesus, which meant *savior*. By naming Jesus, Joseph would become his foster father and connect Jesus to the line of David, from which the Messiah was promised. Joseph awoke and did as the

angel said, taking Mary into his home in Nazareth as his wife.

Luke's Gospel tells us that Jesus was born in Bethlehem. The Roman emperor Caesar Augustus called for a census of the whole empire, requiring all people to return to the place of their birth to record their names. Joseph, who belonged to the house of David, returned to Bethlehem, the city of David. Mary went with him, even though she was about to give birth to her baby.

5. Joseph and Mary arrived in Bethlehem but could not find lodging. They took refuge in a shelter for animals. There Mary gave birth to Jesus—
the Savior, the Messiah, the Son of God.

Luke's story of Jesus' birth proclaims that Jesus was the promised Messiah and Son of God. But the story also suggests that some people would have no room for this Savior in their hearts.

When Joseph and Mary arrived in Bethlehem, so many others crowded the city for the census that there was no room in any inn. But Joseph had to find a place for Mary because she was about to give birth to her baby. So they took refuge in a shelter for animals—a cave on the side of a hill. There the baby was born. Mary wrapped him in the swaddling clothes she had prepared for him. She laid him in his first cradle, a manger.

Many shepherds in that area spent the nights watching over their sheep. An angel appeared to them, telling them the good news of Jesus' birth: "This day in David's city a savior has been born to you, the Messiah and

Lord" (Luke 2:11). The shepherds, like the many poor and outcast people who later heard Jesus teaching, believed the good news. Then many angels suddenly appeared, praising God and singing (Luke 2:14),

> Glory to God in high heaven,
> peace on earth to those on whom
> his favor rests.

The shepherds went to Bethlehem and found Mary, Joseph, and the baby.

Luke's story tells us that Jesus was the Son of God and the Messiah as the angels announced. But Jesus was a Messiah who would suffer and die to give all people new life, a Messiah who would not lead armies but would reach out to the poor and the outcast—to everyone.

Every year on December 25, we celebrate Christmas in remembrance of Jesus' birth.

6. The story of the Magi from the East coming to worship Jesus in Bethlehem shows that Jesus was the Savior of the people of the whole world.

The Gospel of Matthew tells the story of the learned men from the East who came to worship the newborn Jesus in Bethlehem. These learned men studied the heavenly bodies. They were called *Magi,* a name originally given to priests of Persia (the country now known as Iran). In the story, the Magi saw a new star rising in the heavens and decided to follow it.

When the Magi arrived in Jerusalem asking for the newborn king of the Jews, whose star they had seen, their questions upset King Herod, who thought he was the only king of the Jews. The king asked his priests and scribes where the Messiah was to be born. They told him in Bethlehem of Judea.

The Magi left Jerusalem and continued to follow the star. When the star finally stood still over the house where Jesus was, they were overjoyed. In the house they found Jesus with his mother, Mary. They did homage before the baby and presented him gifts of gold, frankincense, and myrrh. Then they returned to their own country.

This story shows that Jesus' coming was important to the people of the whole world. The Magi came from a land that was not awaiting a Messiah. To these learned men, Jesus was worthy of adoration, despite the poverty of his birthplace. We call the event in this story the Epiphany, which means the *showing forth* or *manifestation.* We celebrate it on January 6.

Old Testament writers, after the Jewish exile, described the Messiah as a universal king, a king to whom all nations would come (Isaiah 60:1-3;5-6):

> Rise up in splendor! Your light has come,
>   the glory of the Lord shines upon you.
> See, darkness covers the earth,
>   and thick clouds cover the peoples;
> But upon you the Lord shines,
>   and over you appears his glory.
> Nations shall walk by your light,
>   and kings by your shining radiance.
> . . . the riches of the sea shall be emptied out before you,
>   the wealth of nations shall be brought to you.
> Caravans of camels shall fill you,
>   dromedaries from Midian and Ephah;
> All from Sheba shall come
>   bearing gold and frankincense,
>   and proclaiming the praises of the Lord.

When people celebrate the Epiphany today, they sometimes use words from this Old Testament writing in their prayers.

7. Around the age of thirty, Jesus left home to begin his mission. John the Baptist was preaching at this time, calling people to change their lives and prepare for the coming of the Messiah. Jesus had John baptize him. This event marked the beginning of Jesus' ministry, and it pointed to Jesus as the Messiah who would suffer for God's people.

We know very little about Jesus' life as a young child or a boy growing up. It seems that he did not draw any special attention to himself in the quiet atmosphere of his town. Only once after his early childhood are we shown signs of his future greatness. This was the time when Jesus, at the age of twelve, astonished the learned men in the temple of Jerusalem by discussing religious questions with exceptional depth for a boy of his age (Luke 2:41-50). His parents, too, were amazed at his behavior and his reply to their questions: "Did you not know I had to be in my Father's house?"

Only Matthew and Luke include stories about Jesus' infancy and childhood in their Gospels. But all of the Gospels mark the beginning of Jesus' ministry with his Baptism by John the Baptizer. John preached in the desert of Judea. He proclaimed the coming of the Messiah and urged people to prepare for this and change their hearts. When people took his words seriously and agreed to live as he suggested, he baptized them, submerging them in the waters of the River Jordan as they confessed their sins.

Around the age of thirty, Jesus left the home where he had lived and worked with Joseph and Mary. He came down from Nazareth in Galilee to the place where John was baptizing at the River Jordan. He, too, chose to go through the Baptism as many of John's followers had done. After Jesus came up out of the water, a voice from heaven said, "You are my beloved Son. On you my favor rests" (Mark 1:11).

These words pointed Jesus out as God's Son. They also told something important to people who knew the Hebrew Scriptures. For these words came from a song written by the prophet called Second Isaiah—a song describing the servant of Yahweh who would suffer for his people. John the Baptist, being a prophet, recognized that the great event he had been proclaiming had arrived. He set out to tell everyone about it.

8. Jesus called people to follow him. Twelve of his followers, some of them fishermen, became his apostles.

In Palestine in Jesus' time, people who knew and taught the laws of Jewish religion were called rabbis or teachers. They went throughout the country, teaching people and gathering students.

After his Baptism in the River Jordan, Jesus of Nazareth began to teach and to gather followers. People sometimes addressed him as "Rabbi" or "Teacher," just as they did other teachers of the time. But Jesus' teaching was quite different from the teaching of others. He spoke from his own authority rather than explaining the opinions and thoughts of other teachers.

Meeting Jesus was an extraordinary experience. His deeply human character moved those who met him face-to-face. He impressed those open-minded people who were willing to listen to his message and prepared to take seriously his words, his deeds, and his marvelous ability to see into the hearts of human beings.

Nathanael was one person Jesus impressed. Jesus called Nathanael a sincere and honest Israelite. When Nathanael asked Jesus how he knew him, Jesus replied that he had seen Nathanael under a fig tree even before Nathanael's friend Philip had brought him to Jesus. Nathanael realized that Jesus was an extraordinary person. He said, "Rabbi, you are the Son of God; you are the king of Israel" (John 1:49).

The Gospel according to Mark (1:16-20) tells the story of how Jesus called his disciples:

> As he made his way along the Sea of Galilee, he observed Simon and his brother Andrew casting their nets into the sea; they were fishermen. Jesus said to them, "Come after me; I will make you fishers of men." They immediately abandoned their nets and became his followers. Proceeding a little farther along, he caught sight of James, Zebedee's son, and his brother John. They too were in their boat putting their nets in order. He summoned them on the spot. They abandoned their father Zebedee, who was in the boat with the hired men, and went off in his company.

Soon others joined this company, forming a fairly solid group of followers. These followers were the disciples of Jesus, who left behind their families, their jobs, and their whole way of life in order to listen to Jesus and imitate him. Most of them were plain working people who earned a living by fishing or tilling their small plots of farmland. Twelve of these disciples were chosen by Jesus for a special role. They were to be the apostles—the people sent out to share and continue Jesus' own work. Their names were: "Simon, now known as Peter, and his brother Andrew; James, Zebedee's son, and his brother John; Philip and Bartholomew, Thomas and Matthew the tax collector; James, son of Alphaeus, and Thaddeus; Simon the Zealot Party member, and Judas Iscariot" (Matthew 10:2-4).

9. Jesus traveled from place to place in Palestine in the company of his apostles. He proclaimed the beginning of a new era for all.

Together with those he had chosen, Jesus moved from place to place in Palestine, proclaiming the beginning of a new era, which he described as the reign or kingdom of God. All could belong to it, even sinners and those who had gone astray. To make his message clearer, Jesus told a story (Luke 15:11-20):

A man had two sons. The younger of them said to his father, "Father, give me the share of the estate that is coming to me." So the father divided up the property. Some days later this younger son collected all his belongings and went off to a distant land, where he squandered his money on dissolute living. After he had spent everything, a great famine broke out in that country and he was in dire need. So he attached himself to one of the propertied class of the place, who sent him to his farm to take care of the pigs. He longed to fill his belly with the husks that were fodder for the pigs, but no one made a move to give him anything. Coming to his senses at last, he said: "How many hired hands at my father's place have more than enough to eat, while here I am starving! I will break away and return to my father, and say to him, Father, I have sinned against God and against you; I no longer deserve to be called your son. Treat me like one of your hired hands." With that he set off for his father's

house. While he was still a long way off, his father caught sight of him and was deeply moved. He ran out to meet him, threw his arms around his neck, and kissed him.

Jesus was trying to tell people that God is like that father. With affection and love, he welcomes back those who wish to return to him, even if they have made many mistakes.

Jesus' message was an evangel, a gospel; both words mean a message of good news. His message was the happy announcement that God loves and welcomes all those who turn to him. But Jesus was also very demanding on those who wished to follow him. It was not enough to love God; one also had to love God with one's whole heart and mind. It was not enough to love one's friends; one also had to love all human beings, even one's enemies. It was not enough to obey the law; one also had to act with a pure heart and an upright attitude.

One time a young man approached Jesus and asked him, "Teacher, what good must I do to possess everlasting life?" Jesus replied, "Keep the commandments." The young man said, "I have kept all these." Jesus replied, "If you seek perfection, go, sell your possessions, and give to the poor. You will then have treasure in heaven. Afterward come back and follow me" (Matthew 19: 16-22). Jesus demands great personal sacrifice from those who wish to be his disciples.

10. The Gospels tell us not only of Jesus' words but also of his deeds. The stories of his miracles are signs of God's love, and they invite us to have faith. In one story, Jesus fed five thousand people with five loaves and two fishes.

The authority of Jesus' teaching brought many people to hear him. Mark's Gospel tells about crowds of people gathering around Jesus. To him came the sick, the lame, the blind, and in one story, the hungry.

When the story of his feeding the five thousand (Mark 6:34-44) began, Jesus' friends had been away spreading his teaching. When they returned, Jesus said to them, "Come by yourselves to an out-of-the-way place and rest a little" (Mark 6:31). Jesus and the apostles then went by boat to a deserted place, but people saw them going and arrived at the place on foot ahead of them. The good will of the crowd moved Jesus to pity, and he taught them at length. He spoke so long that the disciples finally said to him, "This is a deserted place and it is already late. Why do you not dismiss them so

that they can go to the crossroads and villages around here and buy themselves something to eat?" Jesus replied, "You give them something to eat." His disciples looked at each other with embarrassment. They had only five loaves of bread and two fish, hardly enough for themselves. They wondered how they could feed the whole crowd. Jesus said to them, "Bring me your food and have the people sit down." Then Jesus blessed and broke the loaves and gave them to his disciples to distribute. He did the same with the fish. The people had all they wanted to eat. And the disciples filled twelve baskets with leftovers.

This is just one of the miracle stories in the Gospels. The evangelist John called the miracle stories in his Gospel *signs*. In these stories, Jesus healed the sick, restored Lazarus to life, and fed crowds of hungry people. Some people in these stories saw Jesus' wondrous deeds and believed in him. Others misunderstood. But all of these signs pointed to who Jesus was—a man in whom the reality of God's presence broke into the world.

The signs pointed to Jesus as the only real and proper support for human beings on their journey through life. In the miracle stories, Jesus confronted evils and caused joy and praise of God. For the early Church, these stories expressed believers' faith in Jesus as one sent from God—as the Son of God.

Indeed, the greatest miracle was Jesus himself. In him God became a human being. In his resurrection God showed us a whole new kind of humanity.

11. Jesus' ministry came to a climax in Jerusalem. There he ate a special meal with his twelve apostles. During the meal, he gave them and all who later followed him the greatest sign of his love: the Eucharist.

Jesus went to Jerusalem near the time of the Passover, the Jews' greatest feast. Later on, Christians would celebrate Holy Week—recalling the passion, death, and resurrection of Jesus—during this same time. Going up to Jerusalem brought Jesus into conflict with those who thought his teaching threatened the law. For Jesus, to go to Jerusalem meant to face death.

Jesus wanted to celebrate the Passover with his closest disciples—the twelve apostles. In the course of the festivities, Jesus gave the apostles and all his followers the greatest sign of his love: the Eucharist. This gift would ensure Jesus' presence among his followers for all time to come. Here is how St. Paul described the institution of the Eucharist (1 Corinthians 11:23-25):

> The Lord Jesus on the night in which he was betrayed took bread, and after he had given thanks, broke it and said, "This is my body, which is for you. Do this in remembrance of me." In the same way, after the supper, he took the cup, saying, "This cup is the new covenant in my blood. Do this, whenever you drink it, in remembrance of me."

The Eucharist was the greatest sign of Jesus' love for his disciples because it represented the death he would accept and suffer for all human beings. Since then, Christians have remembered and made present Jesus' sacrifice by eating the bread and drinking the wine in the Eucharist as he commanded. The apostles did not fully grasp the meaning of Jesus' words and actions at their last supper with him. But they cherished in their hearts the words Jesus spoke. They believed them to be true.

The authority with which Jesus taught seemed to some people to threaten the laws of God on which Judaism was based. His teaching upset many people. His words turned these people's own ideas, habits, and convictions upside down. And that was what happened with the religious leaders of the Jewish people. If they had accepted Jesus' teaching, their own authority would have come into question. In Jerusalem, the conflict between Jesus and some of the Jewish leaders became so great that they wished his death.

While Jesus and his apostles were eating their last meal together, one of the apostles slipped away. It was Judas, who was about to betray him. Judas went to the leaders of the Jewish people and offered to help them capture Jesus. He knew that Jesus, after the meal was over, would retire to a hillside near Jerusalem. There in an olive garden called Gethsemane he would pray. Informed of this, the high priest made preparations to arrest Jesus.

12. **Jesus was arrested, tried, and condemned to death. An innocent victim, he shed his blood for the sins of all human beings. On the Friday before Passover, he died on a cross between two other condemned men.**

A crowd came to arrest Jesus in the garden and brought him to the high priest, who was meeting with the council of Jewish leaders. Although witnesses under oath spoke falsely against Jesus, the leaders could find no real charge against him. Then they asked Jesus if he was the Messiah, the Son of God. This was the heart of the matter. Because Jesus answered yes, he was condemned to death.

There was one remaining problem for the leaders, however—a big one. Israel was under Roman law, and according to Roman law and practice, they could not put a person to death. The death sentence had to be approved and carried out by the Roman authorities. The Roman governor, Pontius Pilate, realized that the charges against Jesus were false, but he feared angering the people; so he confirmed the death sentence. Jesus was condemned to crucifixion.

Jesus' disciples, who had seen him arrested, were afraid for their own lives. Only

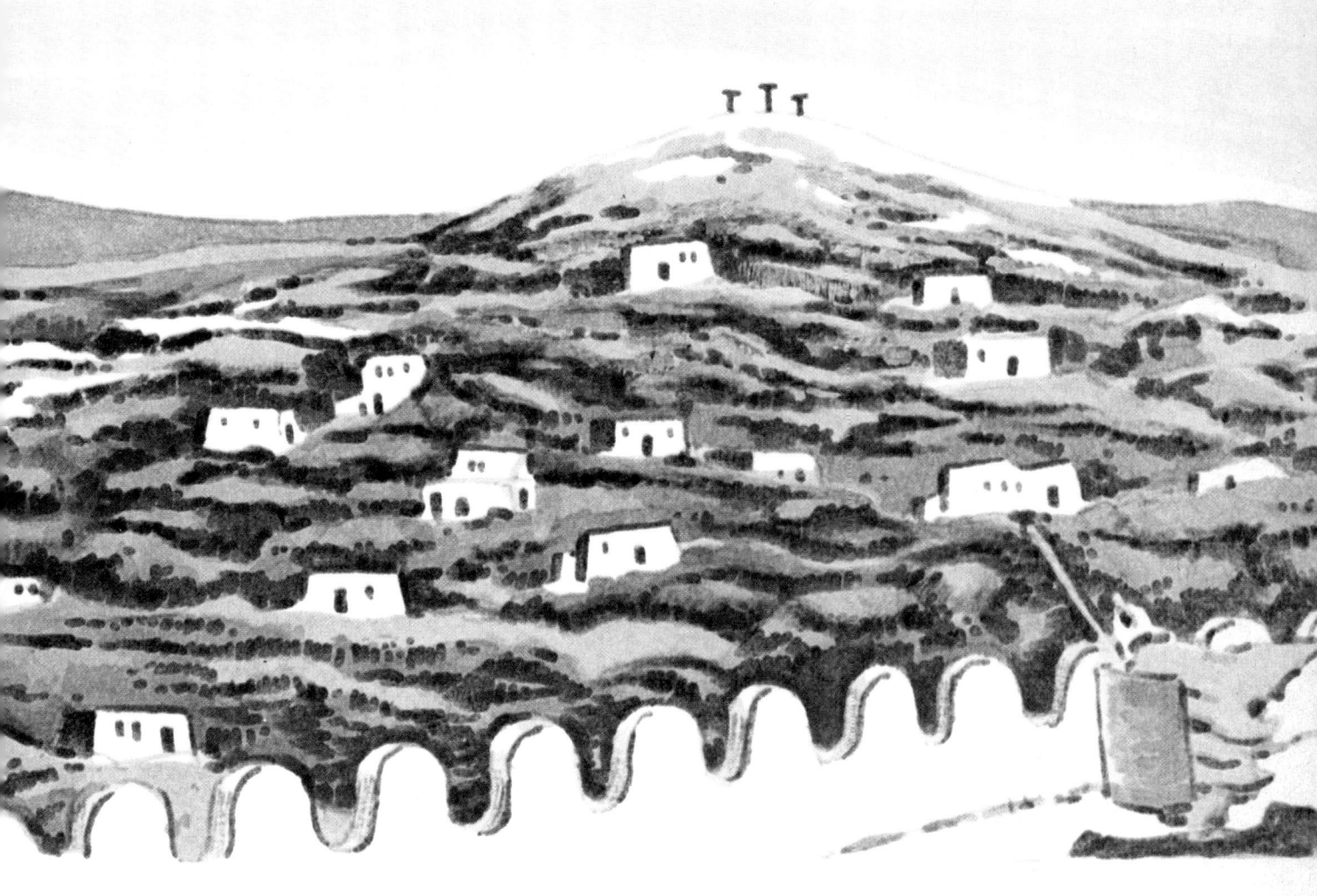

the apostle John followed Jesus to his place of death and stayed with Jesus' mother, Mary, during the crucifixion.

Death by crucifixion was the punishment reserved by the Romans for slaves and despised criminals—including political rebels opposed to Roman rule. It was considered a shameful way to die. So around 10:00 A.M. on the Friday before Passover, a pitiful-looking procession of Roman soldiers and three condemned men, including Jesus, set out toward a hillside named Calvary outside the gates of Jerusalem. Around noon Jesus was nailed to his cross, which was then raised up and planted firmly in the ground. Weakened by all the suffering he had endured, Jesus did not last long on the cross. Around 3:00 P.M. he cried out for the last time to his heavenly Father and died.

During the time between his arrest and his death, Jesus did not say a great deal. But he was not completely silent. Mark's Gospel shows us Jesus' determination to speak the truth (Mark 14:61-62):

> Once again the high priest interrogated him: "Are you the Messiah, the Son of the Blessed One?" Then Jesus answered: "I am; and you will see the Son of Man seated at the right hand of the Power and coming with the clouds of heaven."

"The Blessed One" and "the Power" were terms the Jews used in place of God's name, Yahweh, because they thought God's name was too holy to utter. Jesus was saying that he was the Son of God, whose death would be the victory of salvation for all human beings.

After he had died on the cross, Jesus was taken down. His body, properly prepared, was then laid in a tomb that a friend, Joseph of Arimathea, had provided.

13. After three days, the Father raised Jesus up to new life. This was the first Easter. All human beings share in this feast, which celebrates new life for humanity.

When the women came to Jesus' tomb on the first Easter morning, they found it empty. God had raised up Jesus, who had been crucified. In dying on the cross, Jesus gave his life for the salvation of human beings. His resurrection fully revealed his power as Redeemer, Savior, and Messiah of all humanity. The resurrection showed that the love he preached was indeed life-giving.

In his resurrection Jesus freed all human beings from death. He was the firstborn of a new humanity—a humanity that shared the very life of God. Many recognized Jesus as the Son of God and gathered together in his name. This community of believers became the Church.

Jesus' resurrection erased from his disciples all fear of death. They now knew that their leader had overcome death and that they too would return to life after their death. The resurrection made concrete and real all the things that the earlier prophets had tried to predict by using vivid images and words. They had said that in the age of the Messiah, suffering, crying, and all the evils afflicting human beings would disappear. They were

trying to describe a totally new situation for human beings.

Here is how one prophet in the Old Testament had tried to describe the new and totally different situation that would result from the victorious life of the Messiah (Isaiah 35:1-9):

> The desert and the parched land will exult; the steppe will rejoice and bloom. They will bloom with abundant flowers, and rejoice with joyful song. . . . Say to those whose hearts are frightened: Be strong, fear not! Here is your God, he comes with vindication; with divine recompense he comes to save you. Then will the eyes of the blind be opened, the ears of the deaf be cleared. Then will the lame leap like a stag, then the tongue of the dumb will sing. . . . A highway will be there, called the holy way; no one unclean may pass over it, nor fools go astray on it. No lion will be there, nor beast of prey go up to be met upon it. It is for those with a journey to make, and on it the redeemed will walk.

14. The risen Jesus appeared to his friends—to Mary Magdalene, to two disciples on the way to Emmaus, and to the apostles who had returned to their work as fishermen. Jesus ate a meal of fish with the apostles and asked them to bear witness to his resurrection to all people. Peter, he said, was to be the shepherd of his flock.

Although Jesus' disciples had abandoned him in his time of suffering, he knew that they still loved him and were in mourning for him. He showed himself to them so that they could share in the joy of his new life and witness to others.

According to John's Gospel, the risen Jesus first appeared to Mary Magdalene. Early Sunday morning, she went to the tomb where Jesus was buried. To her surprise, she found the tomb empty. Frightened, she hurried to tell the apostles Peter and John. They rushed to the tomb and also found it empty. Amazed, they returned to their lodgings. But Mary stayed and wept. A person approached her and asked, "Woman, why are you weeping?" Mary pleaded to know where Jesus' body had been taken. She thought she was talking to the gardener and said, "Sir, if you are the one who carried him off, tell me where you have laid him and I will take him away." Then the man said simply, "Mary!" When she heard the man speak her name, she recognized that Jesus was standing before her (John 20:1-18).

In the early afternoon of the very same day, two disciples were on their way to Emmaus, a town about seven miles away from Jerusalem. A stranger approached and joined them on the trip. Noticing their sad faces, he asked them, "What are you discussing as you go your way?" Surprised to find out that the stranger did not seem to know anything about the events that had taken place in Jerusalem the past few days, they told him about Jesus of Nazareth and his recent crucifixion. "We were hoping," they said, "that he was the one who would set Israel free." The stranger exclaimed, "What little sense you have! How slow you are to believe all that the prophets have announced! Did not the Messiah have to undergo all this so as to enter into his glory?" Then the stranger explained passages of the Old Testament referring to the Messiah, showing them that the Messiah had to suffer such things. The two disciples invited the stranger to dine with them when they reached Emmaus. At the meal, the stranger took bread, blessed it, broke it, and distributed it to them. In the breaking of the bread the disciples recognized their beloved Jesus. But he suddenly vanished from their sight (Luke 24:13-35).

On another occasion Jesus appeared to his apostles by the Sea of Tiberias and prepared a meal for them on a charcoal fire. He took bread and gave it to them and did the same with fish. Among those present at the Sea of Tiberias were John, who quickly recognized Jesus, and Peter. Jesus told Peter he wanted him to be the shepherd of his sheep or, in other words, the leader and guide of his Church.

The disciples experienced Jesus near, alive, present with them. The risen Lord Jesus returned to his heavenly Father, from whom he had come.

15. The story of Jesus did not end with his return to the Father. It continued with the community of his disciples, known as the Church. The apostles were in charge of the community. They asked Jesus' guidance and chose a new companion to take the place of Judas Iscariot.

The story of Jesus did not end with his return to God, his Father. The risen Jesus was present with his disciples in a new way. They realized that they had been witnesses to the greatest event in history and that they were the first members of a great people—the People of God, or, the Church. The apostles, in particular, held a special place. They were the eyewitnesses of Jesus' resurrection, the authorized preachers of his message.

There had been twelve apostles until Judas betrayed Jesus and left their ranks. So the first job of the new community was to choose

another apostle to take the place of Judas. It was important that there be twelve apostles because these men were supposed to symbolize the twelve tribes of Israel. So the group of disciples, now numbering about 120, held a meeting to choose a new apostle. Peter, the new head of the little community, stood up and addressed them. He reminded them how Judas had betrayed Jesus and then committed suicide. Then he said, "It is entirely fitting . . . that one of those who was of our company while the Lord Jesus moved among us, from the baptism of John until the day he was taken up from us, should be named as witness with us to his resurrection" (Acts 1:21-22).

Two people met the requirements: Joseph (called Barsabbas, also known as Justus) and Matthias. The community decided to pray so that they would know which one to choose: "Oh Lord, you read the hearts of men. Make known to us which of these two you choose for this apostolic ministry, replacing Judas." They then drew lots and the winner was Matthias. He became the new twelfth apostle—a witness to the resurrection of Jesus.

16. **The Holy Spirit, promised by Jesus, descended upon the disciples of Jesus. Filled with this Spirit, they hurried into the streets to proclaim the salvation brought by Jesus. People from many nations, who spoke different languages, understood them. Three thousand people were baptized that day.**

The election of Matthias brought again to twelve the leaders of the Christian community. Fifty days after the resurrection of Jesus, these twelve disciples gathered in prayer with Mary, Jesus' mother. The Holy Spirit descended upon them. Luke compared the Spirit's coming to the rush of a strong wind followed by a flaming fire that separated and touched each of them. Jesus had promised that he would send his Spirit when he had returned to his Father.

The Spirit filled the disciples with new courage, making them become active witnesses to Jesus. Indeed, the Holy Spirit makes every Christian a witness to Jesus.

When the Spirit descended upon the disciples, many people of Jerusalem came to see what was going on. Peter stood up before a great crowd and proclaimed that God had raised up Jesus, who had been crucified.

At that time, a great feast was being celebrated in Jerusalem. Members of the Jewish religion from many parts of the world were in the city: Iranians, Syrians, Greeks, Egyptians, Africans, and Romans. All of these people who listened to the disciples of Jesus understood them, as if the disciples were speaking the various languages of these people. The disciples seemed to be speaking a universal language for all human beings that went straight to the heart and was immediately understood.

But some onlookers were doubtful. They thought the disciples of Jesus were babbling away because they were drunk. Peter said to them (Acts 2:14-33):

> You who are Jews, indeed all of you staying in Jerusalem! Listen to what I have to say. You must realize that these men are not drunk.... Jesus the Nazorean was a man whom God sent to you with miracles, wonders, and signs as his credentials.... He was delivered up by the set purpose and plan of God; you even made use of pagans to crucify and kill him. God freed him from death's bitter pangs, however, and raised him up again, for it was impossible that death should keep its hold on him. David [spoke] of him...thus proclaiming beforehand the resurrection of the Messiah. This is the Jesus God has raised up, and we are his witnesses. Exalted at God's right hand, he first received the promised Holy Spirit from the Father, then poured this Spirit out on us. This is what you now see and hear.

Peter's words moved many to ask, "What are we to do?" Peter replied, "You must reform and be baptized, each one of you, in the name of Jesus Christ, that your sins may be forgiven; then you will receive the gift of the Holy Spirit" (Acts 2:38). Around three thousand people were baptized that day and joined the ranks of Jesus' followers.

17. One day Peter and John met a crippled man at the temple gate, and Peter cured him in the name of Jesus. Peter proclaimed the good news of the risen Jesus to all who saw this event, but the temple priests had the two apostles arrested.

The new Christian community had grown to about three thousand people. Every day they gathered around the apostles to hear what these men had learned from Jesus. Then they all went to the temple to praise God.

One afternoon, Peter and John were on their way to the temple. They were stopped at the gate by a poor man, paralyzed from birth, who sat there every day to beg alms. The two apostles were deeply moved. Peter said to this man, "I have neither silver nor gold, but what I have I give you! In the name of Jesus Christ the Nazorean, walk!" (Acts 3:6). Then Peter pulled him to his feet, and the man's feet and ankles suddenly became strong. He entered the temple walking, jumping around, and praising God.

People in the temple area recognized this

man as the one who used to sit begging at the gate. They were amazed at what they saw, and they excitedly rushed over to Peter and John. Peter saw a good opportunity to tell them about Jesus, and so he began to speak (Acts 3:12-26):

> Fellow Israelites . . . why do you stare at us as if we had made this man walk by some power or holiness of our own? . . . The God of our fathers has glorified his Servant Jesus. . . . You put to death the Author of life. But God raised him from the dead, and we are his witnesses. It is his name, and trust in his name, that has strengthened the limbs of this man whom you see and know well. . . . Yet I know, my brothers, that you acted out of ignorance, just as your leaders did. God has brought to fulfillment by this means what he announced long ago through all the prophets: that his Messiah would suffer. Therefore, reform your lives! Turn to God, that your sins may be wiped away! . . . When God raised up his servant, he sent him to you first to bless you by turning you from your evil ways.

While Peter was speaking, some temple priests joined the audience. When they heard his final remarks, they were enraged. Just as they had done with Jesus, they had Peter and John arrested and put into prison. But many of those who heard Peter's speech believed in his message and joined the Christian community. There were now about five thousand members.

18. We often hear mention of the Sanhedrin in the stories of Jesus and his apostles. The Sanhedrin was an assembly of the leaders of the Jewish people, made up of priests, scribes, and well-to-do citizens called elders.

The Sanhedrin was an assembly of the leaders of the Jewish people, and it met several times a year, or whenever its more important members called a meeting. The members of the Sanhedrin would meet in a room of the temple or the synagogue, the Jewish house of prayer and worship, in order to reach important decisions about religious matters, about the observance of the Jewish law, or about civil life. Sanhedrins existed in all the main towns of Palestine, but the one in Jerusalem was obviously the most important because Jerusalem was the capital city.

The Sanhedrin of Jerusalem was really like a congress or parliament. It made important decisions, not only for Jerusalem, but for the whole region. It was composed of seventy-one persons, who met in a hall in the southwest section of the temple. The seventy-one members came from three groups: the priests, the scribes, and the elders.

The priests had always held a very important place in the history of Israel. They presided over religious services in the temple. According to Jewish law, they had the task of explaining the holy writings to the people. At their head was the chief high priest, who was also the head of the whole Jewish nation. Not

all priests were members of the Sanhedrin, of course—only the chief high priest and those who had held that office before him. The latter often had more power and authority than the high priest who was currently in office.

The scribes had great influence during the time of Jesus. They were learned Jews who had gradually taken over from the priests the task of explaining the law. After a long period of training, which might last for many years, a scribe was entitled to teach the Jewish law and to resolve questions and disputes about it. Thus the scribes had become a powerful group of people with great control over the Jewish law. Only a few scribes, regarded as outstanding because of their learning or their family connections, were able to be members of the Sanhedrin. Jesus sometimes had very harsh words for scribes who forgot that the law was intended to help people live their faith in God.

The elders were well-to-do landowners and merchants who were heads of large family groups. Election to the Sanhedrin meant recognition of their success in the life of Jewish society.

19. The Sanhedrin met to pass judgment on Peter and John. When asked to explain the miracle, Peter told the Sanhedrin that Jesus was responsible for the cure, and that all should look to him for salvation. The Sanhedrin sternly warned the apostles not to talk about Jesus again, but Peter and John refused to obey.

Before we discussed the Sanhedrin in the last section, we left Peter and John in prison after the cure of the crippled man. The next morning, the members of the Sanhedrin met to pass judgment on the two apostles, who were led in for questioning (Acts 4:5-22). This was an important moment because it represented a major exchange between the Jewish authorities and the followers of Jesus.

"By what power or in whose name have men of your stripe done this?" asked the Sanhedrin. Peter, filled with the Holy Spirit, gave this reply:

> Leaders of the people! Elders! . . . It was done in the name of Jesus Christ the Nazorean whom you crucified and whom God raised from the dead. . . . This Jesus is "the stone rejected by you the builders which has become the cornerstone." There is no salvation in anyone else, for there is no other name in the whole world given to men by which we are to be saved.

The members of the Sanhedrin were amazed. Not only had these men worked a miracle; now they were talking with boldness and self-assurance, even though they were not highly educated people. Their power and influence could not be denied. But the Sanhedrin thought that Peter and John had to be kept in their proper place, even if these men did not actually deserve punishment.

Actually, it would have been unwise for the Sanhedrin to punish the apostles because the people were on their side. So the apostles were told sternly not to talk about Jesus. But it is hard to keep quiet if one believes that one is speaking the truth and has something important to say. As Peter and John told the Sanhedrin, "Judge for yourselves whether it is right in God's sight for us to obey you rather than God. Surely we cannot help speaking of what we have heard and seen" (Acts 4:19-20).

20. As the Church began to take more definite shape, different people took charge of various functions. Three lasting functions were those of bishop, priest, and deacon.

The most important people in the newly born Christian community were, of course, the twelve apostles. Their chief function was to testify to the life, death, and resurrection of Jesus and to proclaim his message. They were to convert people and baptize them.

Paul's first letter to the Corinthians describes the organization of the early Church (1 Corinthians 12:28): "God has set up in the church first apostles, second prophets, third teachers, then miracle workers, healers, assistants, administrators, and those who speak in tongues." Some of the functions described here still remain, and some were merged with others as the or-

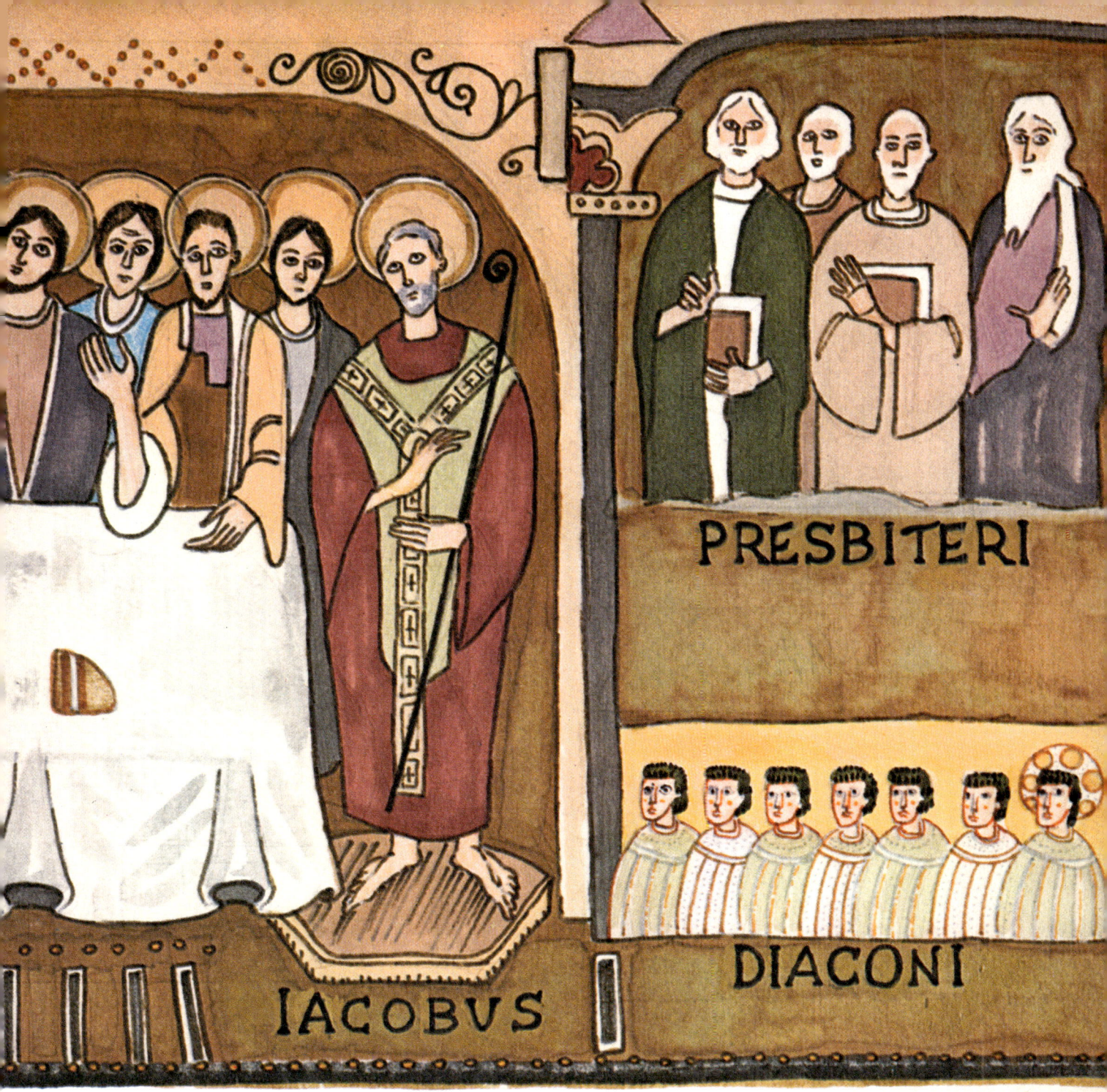

ganization of the Church took more definite shape. Three lasting functions were those of bishop, priest, and deacon.

Apparently, the term *overseers* (or *bishops*) was at first used interchangeably with the term *elders* (*presbyters* or *priests*). These people were the directors of local churches. They kept watch over the whole local church community under the guidance of the Holy Spirit (Acts 20:28).

Gradually, the head of each local group took on more authority, until he alone was called bishop. Parishes developed within his community, with priests as their heads. These priests were under the bishop's charge.

Deacons ministered to the everyday needs of people in the Church community. They gave out alms to those in need and assisted the bishops in many ways. Later, we shall read about Stephen, one of the first deacons.

Women, too, played an important role in the early Church; for example, deaconesses, or women deacons, helped in the community. Several women who had associated with Jesus were major figures in the Church. Mary gave birth to Jesus and was the first to believe in him. And it was Mary Magdalene who first saw the risen Jesus and proclaimed his resurrection to the apostles (John 20:11-18).

21. Let's imagine the story of a young man whom we will call Alexander. Born a Greek in Corinth, he had converted to the Jewish religion and come to Jerusalem to celebrate the feasts of Passover and Weeks. Hearing Peter's speech at

Pentecost, he approached a disciple for further information. He decided to become a follower of Jesus and was finally baptized.

We can imagine the life of a young man who might have been among the many people listening to Peter's speeches on Pentecost. We will call him Alexander. Born into a well-to-do Greek family in Corinth, a major city in Greece, Alexander received a good education in Greek thought and religion. But he still did not feel satisfied with life. One day he noticed people gathering in a place known as a synagogue, and he decided to find out what exactly they were doing and why. He found himself in an assembly of Jews listening to one of the elders read the Sacred Scriptures and comment on them. He heard about a loving God who was very different from the gods of the Greeks. Soon Alexander was going to the synagogue every Saturday, and he eventually decided to convert to the Jewish religion.

Continuing to study his new religion, Alexander learned that its most important city was Jerusalem, with its great temple. Every year two major feasts, Passover and Pentecost (or the feast of Weeks), were celebrated there by thousands of Jews from all over the world. Alexander decided to join the celebration of Passover this year, and so he traveled to Jerusalem. But this year a strange event had upset things a bit. A certain man named Jesus, whom many people spoke well of, had been put to death.

Fifty days after Passover, when Alexander had almost forgotten the name of Jesus, he was still in Jerusalem to celebrate the feast of Pentecost with his companions. Suddenly they heard a loud noise and decided to investigate. Alexander found himself listening to Peter, who was boldly and courageously talking about the deeds and message of Jesus. Alexander gradually began to realize that Jesus was in fact the Messiah, the anointed messenger from God who had been promised to the Jews by the ancient prophets. Alexander approached a disciple for further information and instruction.

After some months of instruction and personal questioning, Alexander was convinced that Jesus was indeed the Messiah. And so Alexander was baptized in the Jordan River, along with many others, and then led off to share in his first eucharistic meal. Having entered the Christian community and received the Holy Spirit, he was now prepared to be a faithful follower of Jesus.

22. Now a Christian, our imaginary Alexander decided to live in the Jerusalem community, where he was converted. He returned to Greece, sold all his possessions, and brought his earnings to the Jerusalem community. Later he was given the task of caring for Bartholomew, a member of the community who was very sick.

Our imaginary story continues. Now a Christian, Alexander thought about his future. He was supposed to go back home and stay there, but he really wanted to live in the new community he had just entered—a community in which he found a spirit of brotherhood and love that he had never experienced before. The members of this community put all their possessions at the disposal of the poorer members, and all lived serenely in the generous spirit of Jesus himself. Alexander decided that he would like to do the same, and so he informed the disciple who had been watching over him and teaching him. Then Alexander set out for Corinth. There he enthusiastically talked to his parents, relatives, and friends about his new faith in Jesus. He told his parents of his desire to sell his share of the inheritance and put the money at the disposal of the

Jerusalem community. His family was amazed and somewhat saddened, but in the end they gave their consent and wished him well. They trusted him because he had always been a respectful, obedient son.

One month after leaving Corinth, Alexander arrived back in Jerusalem. He was overjoyed at being able to embrace all his fellow Christians once again—especially the disciple who had been looking after him. The disciples told him about the great progress the community had made in the months he was away. Tomorrow, they said, the community would meet with Peter and the other apostles to decide what would be done with Alexander's money and goods. At that time, they would also entrust him with a particular task of his own. Alexander went to bed early, anxious to know what his task would be.

The next day, after attending the temple and the eucharistic meal in the evening, Alexander heard about his mission. One of the brothers in the community named Bartholomew was seriously ill. Alexander was to take good care of him, remembering that Jesus was present in a special way in the sick and the suffering. So Alexander spent his days with Bartholomew, showing him great love and attention. He took care of Bartholomew's needs, helped him get to the common meals, and read the sacred scriptures to him. A real friendship developed between them, and the two men thanked Jesus for enabling them to become brothers, even though their pasts had been very different.

23. Stephen, one of the first deacons, was a man filled with faith and the Holy Spirit. Certain Greek-speaking Jewish people envied him and dragged him before the Sanhedrin. Stephen delivered a speech, and the onlookers became so angry that they stoned him to death. He was the first Christian martyr.

Stephen, we learn in the book of Acts, was a good man of deep faith, so he was elected one of the first deacons by the apostles. Filled with grace and power, Stephen began to work miracles among the people. Jews from various places in the Roman empire tried to debate with him, but he always seemed to get the better of the argument.

Envious of him, these people denounced him to the Sanhedrin as one who was speaking blasphemy against Moses and God and criticizing the temple and the Jewish law. When Stephen was brought before the educated men of the Sanhedrin, who claimed to know all about Jewish law, Jewish history, and Jewish religion, he spoke plainly about the history of the Hebrew people (Acts 7:1-60). He explained that God had always been the real guide and liberator of the Hebrew people, but that he had often used means that the people did not understand at first. He told the members of the Sanhedrin that they were the descendants of people who had always stubbornly refused to listen to God, and now they were doing the same thing by having rejected Jesus.

Stephen's words enraged his Jewish listeners. Then Stephen looked up to heaven and saw Jesus at God's right hand. When he told this to the Sanhedrin, the onlookers angrily dragged him outside the city and killed him by stoning.

While he was being stoned to death, Stephen prayed, "Lord Jesus, receive my spirit. . . . do not hold this sin against them" (Acts 7:59-60). Stephen was the first martyr in the Christian community, and his feast is celebrated on December 26, the day after Christmas.

24. One of the queen of Ethiopia's ministers, who believed and practiced the Jewish religion, had come to Jerusalem on a pilgrimage. On his way back home, he met Philip, who explained the Old Testament prophecies to him. The minister realized that Jesus had come for him too, and he asked to be baptized.

God wanted the first Christians to realize that the good news about Jesus was not just for their community. He gradually taught them to bring the Gospel message to more and more people because Jesus had lived, died, and been resurrected for them also.

One day, for example, the Lord told Philip to go at noon along the road that ran from Jerusalem to Gaza (Acts 8:26-40). On the way, Philip came across a carriage in which an important person was seated: a minister of the queen of Ethiopia, a large kingdom in Africa. This minister believed and practiced the Jewish religion, and he had just made the long pilgrimage to Jerusalem that Jews from many regions made. Right now he was reading the book of Isaiah in the Old Testament.

Philip asked the man if he understood what he was reading. The man said he could not, because no one had ever explained it to him. He was reading a passage that talked about a servant of God being humiliated and put to death without saying a word of complaint. Philip explained that Jesus was the person being talked about in this passage. He told the Ethiopian the story of Jesus and his message of salvation. The Ethiopian was deeply moved, realizing that the prophecy had been fulfilled and that salvation had come for him, too. When they came across a body of water on their route, the man asked Philip if he could be baptized. Philip and he went down into the water, and Philip baptized him. When they came out of the water, Philip was suddenly snatched away by the Spirit of the Lord, and the Ethiopian minister saw him no more. But the minister went on his way rejoicing.

25. God showed Peter that there was no longer any real difference between the Jews and pagans and that the commands of the Jewish law about food were no longer binding. Peter accepted the invitation of a Roman centurion to visit his home, and the family of the centurion was baptized.

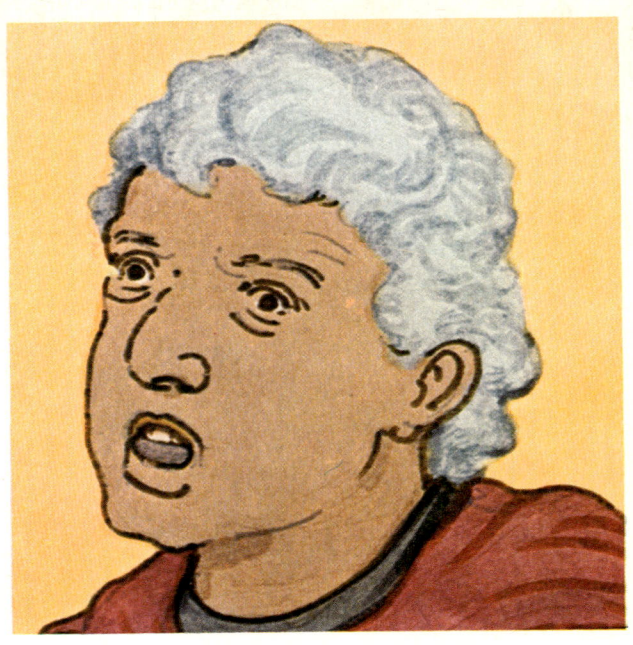

The Christian message had been gradually spreading outside Jerusalem to other surrounding areas. As yet, however, the message of Jesus had not really been proclaimed to anyone except Jews and converts to the Jewish religion. But now the time had come to preach the Gospel to pagans too—that is, to people not of the Jewish religion. God wanted Peter to set an example in this regard (Acts 10:1—11:18). While visiting various Christian communities, Peter stopped over in the city of Joppa (or Jaffa). It was a coastal city not far from Caesarea, where Roman soldiers were stationed. One of the Roman centurions in Caesarea was named Cornelius. He was an upright, God-fearing person, even though he was a pagan, who did not follow Jewish law. He often prayed to God, and now God decided to hear his prayer. While Cornelius was praying one afternoon around three o'clock, he distinctly saw an angel and heard these words: "Cornelius! . . . Your prayers and your generosity have risen in God's sight, and because of them he has remembered you. Send some men to Joppa and summon a certain Simon, known as Peter."

The next day, while those men were on their way to Joppa, Peter himself had a vision while he was at prayer. He had asked for food because he was hungry, and suddenly he saw something like a big sheet or tablecloth coming down from heaven with all sorts of animals in it. Now Jews were not allowed to eat many of them because the Mosaic Law forbade it. Peter heard a voice telling him to kill the animals and eat. Peter said, "Sir, it is unthinkable! I have never eaten anything unclean or impure in my life." Three times the voice replied, "What God has purified, you are not to call unclean." Then the sheet was suddenly drawn up to the sky again.

The main point of the vision was that Peter was supposed to accept the hospitality of an uncircumcised pagan, and that there was no longer any difference between Jews and pagans as far as the message of Jesus was concerned. Pagans, too, should be received into the Church if they accepted Jesus' message; they didn't have to accept the rules of the Mosaic Law.

The servants of Cornelius arrived and extended the centurion's invitation to Peter. Peter had the servants stay with him that night, and the next day they all went to Caesarea and the home of Cornelius. Cornelius told Peter about his vision, and Peter in turn told the centurion's household about Jesus. Peter now realized that God had no special favorites among the peoples of the world.

Before Peter had finished speaking, the Holy Spirit descended on these pagan listeners, and they began to speak in tongues and glorify God. So Peter gave orders for them to be baptized and received into the Christian Church as the first pagan, or Gentile, converts.

26. Christians lived together in community and shared with each other so that no one would be in need. Two people—Ananias and Sapphira—lied about their gift to the Church, and they died. Another person—Simon the magician—tried to buy the power of the apostles.

The group of Jesus' followers grew larger day by day. The Christians went to the temple every day to praise God, and they met in their homes to break bread together, as Jesus had asked them to do in memory of him.

The people in the little Christian community loved and helped each other. No one was ever in want, because many sold their possessions and gave the money to the apostles to use for those in need. Barnabas was one of these generous people. He sold a piece of land and brought all the money to Peter to use for the Christian community.

Ananias and his wife Sapphira (Acts 5:1-11) decided to sell a piece of property. The money from the sale belonged to them as long as they wished to keep it. But they decided to secretly put aside some of the money for themselves, while pretending to give everything to the community. Ananias went to Peter and gave him some money, acting as though it were all the money he had received from the sale.

Peter asked him why he was lying to the Holy Spirit: "You have lied not to men but to God!" At these words, Ananias fell dead. The body was taken away, and later Sapphira came in. When Peter asked her about the sale, she too lied and said that the money Ananias had given Peter was all they had received from the sale. Then she too died. The whole Christian community was astonished and frightened.

Some time later Philip preached in Samaria, and many people were converted and baptized. One such person was Simon the magician, who had been amazing the people there with his magic (Acts 8:9-25). He was quite impressed with the signs and miracles worked by Philip. Soon Peter and John arrived, prayed over the newly baptized people, laid their hands upon them, and thus brought down the Holy Spirit on them. Simon was astounded, and he wanted the power to bring down the Holy Spirit on anyone he laid his hands on. So he offered to give the apostles money if they would give him that power. Peter angrily replied: "May you and your money rot—thinking that God's gift can be bought! You can have no portion or lot in this affair. Your heart is not steadfastly set on God. Reform your evil ways. Pray that the Lord may pardon you for thinking the way you have."

Simon did ask the apostles to pray for him, but ever since that time the word *simony* has been used to describe attempts to buy divine favors with money rather than pleasing God with a true conversion of heart.

27. In this period, Rome began to order the people to worship the emperor as a divine being or as the descendant of a divine being. Other forms of religion also became popular with many people.

While the first Christian communities were being established in Palestine and other eastern parts of the Roman empire, other religious viewpoints were winning followers and influencing each other throughout the Greek and Roman world. With the reign of Caesar Augustus, emperor worship became popular in the eastern part of the empire. The title Augustus (meaning *reverend*) was given to him in 27 B.C., and later a month was named after him (our August). But worship of the living emperor, who was thought to become a god after his death, began in the western part of the empire during the reign of Nero (A.D. 54-68). By the reign of Domitian

(A.D. 81-96), it became the most important part of the Roman state religion. Sacrifices were offered to the emperor, and orgaizations were formed to spread this worship, which was mainly designed to teach political obedience to Rome. This worship had little to do with people's inner search for God, and already existing religions were not banned.

Other religious groups from Egypt, Syria, and Persia tried to explain the meaning of human life and death and to offer some hope of resurrection. Joining these religious groups was not easy. People had to undergo difficult forms of initiation and attend elaborate, complicated ceremonies. Only then could they become real members or priests of these religions dedicated to various gods or goddesses.

In one way or another, many of these cults celebrated the dying and rising of some god or goddess. This mirrored the dying of nature at the end of the year and its glorious rebirth the next spring. It also gave hope to the members of the cult that they too would be able to rise to new life after death. So while the cult of the Roman emperor was mainly political, these other cults were truly religious ones. For they gave expression to the desire for immortality, for everlasting life, that most human beings feel.

28. Saul of Tarsus was a Jew by birth, and he was an active member of the Jewish religion. Saul joined in persecuting Christians until one day on the road to Damascus, he had a vision of Jesus—a vision that would change his whole life.

Now a new figure entered the historical story of the early Church. This disciple of Jesus greatly aided the growth of the Church through his thinking and his missionary activity. He was Saul of Tarsus, the last of the apostles, who later came to be called Paul.

We know very little about Saul's early life, but we get some information from the Acts of the Apostles and from his own letters written later to various Christian communities. Saul was born in Tarsus, a city of Asia Minor, around A.D. 10. His family was Jewish and belonged to the tribe of Benjamin. His father, who may have been a tentmaker by trade, was able to provide him with a good education and also to purchase Roman citizenship for him. This valuable citizenship would prove useful to Saul in later years.

Saul went to Jerusalem and studied under Gamaliel, a famous rabbi, who taught him the religious teachings of the Pharisees. Saul himself never met Jesus of Nazareth during Jesus' ministry, as far as we know. But we do know that his dedication to the Jewish religion made him a fierce enemy of the new Christian community that had arisen after Jesus' death.

We first read of Saul in the New Testament when Stephen, the deacon, is killed. Saul approved of the stoning and went from house to house arresting Christians and sending them off to prison (Acts 8:1-3). Then he decided to get the high priest's permission to go to Damascus to do the same thing, bringing back to Jerusalem the people who were following this "new way" (Acts 9:2).

On the road to Damascus, a town in Syria, Saul had an experience that would completely change his life (Acts 9:3-8):

> As he traveled along and was approaching Damascus, a light from the sky suddenly flashed about him. He fell to the ground and at the same time heard a voice saying, "Saul, Saul, why do you persecute me?" "Who are you, sir?" he asked. The voice answered, "I am Jesus, the one you are persecuting. Get up and go into the city, where you will be told what to do." The men who were traveling with him stood there speechless. They had heard the voice but could see no one. Saul got up from the ground unable to see, even though his eyes were open. They had to take him by the hand and lead him into Damascus.

A new life was about to begin for Saul of Tarsus. He would soon become one of the greatest preachers of Jesus' message and would convert people in many lands.

29. After his encounter with Jesus, Saul arrived in Damascus and was received into the Church by a disciple named Ananias. A few years later, Saul began to preach the Gospel in that city. Certain Jewish people plotted to kill him, but he

managed to escape from Damascus. He visited Jerusalem briefly, where Barnabas introduced him to the apostles. Some Jewish people again plotted to kill him, so Saul headed back home to Tarsus.

After he arrived in Damascus, Saul, who was still blinded, did not eat or drink for three days. A disciple of Jesus in that city named Ananias had a vision in which he was told: "Ananias! ... Go at once to Straight Street, and at the house of Judas ask for a certain Saul of Tarsus. He is there praying" (Acts 9:10-11). Ananias protested strongly because he had heard how viciously Saul had been persecuting Christians. But Jesus told Ananias: "You must go! This man is the instrument I have chosen to bring my name to the Gentiles and their kings and to the people of Israel." Ananias did what he was told and found Saul. He told the still-blinded man, "Saul, my brother, I have been sent by the Lord Jesus who appeared to you on the way here, to help you recover your sight and be filled with the Holy Spirit." Saul immediately regained his sight and was baptized.

After recovering from his experience somewhat, Saul went off to an isolated area in Arabia to pray and to think about his new faith. He returned to Damascus a few years later and began to preach the Gospel message. The Jewish community in that city was astonished because they recognized him as the man who had been such a harsh persecutor of Christians. But they were unable to argue against his proofs that Jesus was in fact the Messiah. Certain Jewish people decided to kill Saul, and so they began to keep close watch on the gates of the city so that Saul could not leave alive. But one night Saul was lowered to the ground outside the city by his Christian followers, and he headed for Jerusalem.

Saul found himself in a difficult situation in Jerusalem, too, because the Christians there were terrified of him. Barnabas took charge of the problem and introduced Saul to the apostles. Barnabas told them all about Saul's vision and conversion, and about his fearless preaching in Damascus of Jesus' word. Soon Saul himself was proving the truth of what Barnabas said; he moved freely around Jerusalem talking about Jesus to all who would listen. He debated Greek-speaking Jewish people, and again some of them plotted to kill him. So his fellow Christians took him down to Caesarea and sent him home to Tarsus for his own protection.

30. After the stoning of Stephen, the Christians were greatly persecuted, and many fled Jerusalem. Antioch, in Syria, became the second home of Christianity. Even non-Jews were attracted to the faith. Barnabas saw the possibility of many conversions and asked Saul to help him. The two men were very successful. Barnabas and Saul later started their mission to other nations. Saul became known as Paul.

After the stoning of Stephen in Jerusalem, many Christians fled the area because the Jews began to persecute them. They went as far as Phoenicia, Cyprus, and Antioch, where they began to proclaim the Christian message to other Jews. And in Antioch, some Christians began to preach to Greeks and converted many of them (Acts 11:19-26).

Informed of this new development, the Church in Jerusalem decided to send

Barnabas to Antioch. Barnabas was very pleased with what he saw, and he urged the Christians in Antioch to keep up the good work they were doing. It seemed to him that many more converts could be made. But Antioch was a big city, and help was needed. Then Barnabas remembered Saul of Tarsus and his great ability as a preacher of the Christian message. So he went to Tarsus and brought Saul back to Antioch with him. For a whole year the two men worked with the Christian community in Antioch and had great success. Indeed, it was in Antioch that the followers of Jesus were first called Christians, and Antioch itself became the second capital of the Christian faith.

Paul and Barnabas began to preach the Gospel message in other regions. At first, they spoke to Jews in their synagogues, attracting many followers. But many pagans came to hear their message, and this made some of the Jews angry. Saul and Barnabas declared, however, that they would preach to all people—pagans and Jews—because the Lord intended them to be "a light to the nations, a means of salvation to the ends of the earth" (Acts 13:47). The pagans rejoiced at these words and thanked God for this message.

During this first missionary journey, Saul began to use the Greek version of his name: Paul. Traveling at first with Barnabas, and then on his own, he began a series of missionary trips through many parts of the Roman empire. Wherever he went, he founded small Christian communities and put them under the care of trustworthy leaders.

31. About fourteen years after Paul's conversion, the first council of the Church took place in Jerusalem. There Paul and Barnabas argued that pagans did not need to be circumcised to become Christians. Peter, the head of the Church, agreed with them.

over the problem with the apostles living there. So, about fourteen years after Paul's conversion, Paul and Barnabas and others traveled to Jerusalem. There they told the Jerusalem Christians what they had been preaching and how the Lord had worked through them to convert many pagans. Many of the Jerusalem Christians praised God for these conversions. But again, some Christians demanded that the new pagan converts be circumcised and that they follow all the Jewish laws. A meeting was held with the apostles, and there was a long discussion. Paul and Barnabas expressed their views. When they had finished, Peter, the head of the apostles and the whole Church, took the

Paul and Barnabas returned to Antioch after their first missionary journey, which had taken them to various places in Asia Minor. They found that the Christian community was still growing. Most of the Christians were Jews, but some were pagans, also called Gentiles. Some Christians from Judea claimed that Gentiles who became Christian had to be circumcised in accordance with the Mosaic Law if they wanted to be saved. This attitude created a serious problem for non-Jews who wished to become Christian.

Paul and Barnabas strongly opposed this view, and eventually the Christian community asked them to go to Jerusalem to talk floor. He said (Acts 15:7-11):

Brothers, you know well enough that from the early days God selected me from your number to be the one from whose lips the Gentiles would hear the message of the gospel and believe. God, who reads the hearts of men, showed his approval by granting the Holy Spirit to them just as he did to us. He made no distinction between them and us, but purified their hearts by means of faith also. Why, then, do you put God to the test by trying to place on the shoulders of these converts a yoke which neither we nor our fathers were able to bear? Our belief is rather that we are saved by the favor of the Lord Jesus and so are they.

Peter's view was accepted, and the apostles informed the Christians in Antioch that they did not have to observe unnecessary Jewish regulations.

The authorities in the Church had spoken out. Their decision was the binding one, even though some Christians continued to insist that Jewish laws still had to be followed. This meeting in Jerusalem, in the presence of Peter and other apostles, was the first Church council. At critical moments in the history of the Church, such councils would indicate to Christians the right road to take.

32. Paul's second trip took him to Athens, Greece, where he spoke about the true God to the learned people of the city. Some were interested in what he had to say, but most found it difficult to believe in the resurrection of Jesus.

After the first council of the Church, Paul and Barnabas returned to Antioch and stayed there until peace and harmony had been restored to the community. Then they set out again, each going in a different direction. Paul traveled through Asia Minor and Macedonia, eventually arriving in Greece. On a rocky hillside near Athens, he made a famous speech. Philosophers and learned men were in his audience because Athens was the great center of philosophy in Greece. Paul delivered this address (Acts 17:22-31):

Men of Athens, I perceive that in every way you are very religious. For as I passed along, and observed the objects of your worship, I found an altar with this inscription, "To an unknown god." What therefore you worship as unknown, this I proclaim to you. The God who made the world and everything in it ... does not live in shrines made by man, nor is he served by human hands, as though he needed anything, since he himself gives to all men life and breath and everything. And he made from one every nation of men to live on all the face of the earth ... that they should seek God, in the hope that they might feel after him and find him. Yet he is not far from each one of us, for "In him we live and move and have our being"; as even some of your poets have said, "For we are indeed his offspring." Being then God's offspring, we ought not to think that the Deity is like gold, or silver, or stone. . . . The times of ignorance God overlooked, but now he commands all men everywhere to repent, because he has fixed a day on which he will judge the world in righteousness by a man whom he has appointed, and of this he has given assurance to all men by raising him from the dead.

When the Athenians heard talk about someone being raised from the dead, some sneered at Paul. Others, however, were curious and asked Paul to speak to them some other time. But these were few in number, and Paul did not make many converts.

More and more, Paul came to feel that he should preach mainly about Jesus, his crucifixion and resurrection, even though people might misunderstand him or be upset by his words. As he himself put it: "Jews demand signs and Greeks seek wisdom, but we preach Christ crucified, a stumbling block to Jews and folly to Gentiles, but to those who are called, both Jews and Greeks, Christ the power of God and the wisdom of God" (1 Corinthians 1:22-24).

33. On his third missionary journey, Paul stopped in Ephesus for several years to instruct the newly formed Christian community. His preaching won many converts and undermined the business of selling statues to people worshiping in the temple of Diana there. The silversmiths stirred up trouble against Paul, who soon continued his journey. On his travels, Paul wrote letters to various Christian communities, such as the one in Corinth.

After leaving Athens, Paul stopped in Corinth, a major center of commerce in Greece. There he argued in the synagogue every sabbath and convinced many Jews and Greeks that Jesus was indeed the Messiah. One night, the Lord spoke to Paul in a vision (Acts 18: 9-10): "Do not be afraid, but speak and do not be silent; for I am with you, and no man shall attack you to harm you; for I have many people in this city." And so Paul stayed in Corinth for a year and a half, preaching the word of God to the people and baptizing new believers.

Then Paul sailed for Syria and stopped briefly at Ephesus. The people there invited him to stay longer, but Paul refused. He did promise, however, to come back again. Paul then made his way back to Antioch and stayed there for a while before setting out on his third missionary journey. This time he kept his promise of staying in Ephesus.

Ephesus was the capital of the Roman province of Asia Minor, a center of contact and communication between the East and the West. About 200,000 people lived in Ephesus, earning their living in the trade of the great port city. Moreover, Ephesus boasted of a great temple to the mother goddess, whom the Greeks called Artemis and the Romans called Diana. This temple was one of the seven wonders of the ancient world. In April and May especially, crowds of pilgrims would flock to the temple to worship the goddess. This meant big business for the silversmiths and others who sold little statues of the goddess, representations of the temple, and amulets with mysterious writing on them. For the great mother goddess was one of the most revered divine figures in the ancient world. Under a variety of names—Diana, Artemis, and Cybele—she was honored as a virgin and a mother.

Paul spent about three years preaching in Ephesus and converted many people to Jesus. Since the people gave up the worship of the mother goddess, this reduced sales of her statues and other objects related to her worship. Paul definitely was bad for business, so one day a man named Demetrius organized a big demonstration against him. There was much arguing back and forth. Finally, the town clerk told the craftsmen to make their complaint in a lawful way and thus put an end to the wild demonstration (Acts 19:23-40).

Paul gave a few words of encouragement to his followers and then set out for Macedonia. But he had heard of arguments among the leaders of the Christian community in Corinth, and so he decided to write them a letter before going there personally. This letter (1 Corinthians) is one of his most famous ones. We can summarize its main points as follows (1 Corinthians, adapted):

My dear Corinthians: I have heard that there are factions and disputes among you. You must be united, trusting not in human wisdom but in the wisdom of the crucified Jesus. The Church must be one, even as Christ is one. I also hear that there are divisions between the rich and the poor when you come together for the eucharistic meal. That is terrible, because the Eucharist symbolizes the oneness of the Church, and it celebrates the mystery of Jesus' death and resurrection. So you must be united, even though you have different jobs and places in the Church. And you must remember that charity (that is, love) is the most important thing—even more important than faith and hope.

34. Returning to Corinth, Paul stayed a few months and converted many people. He was especially concerned about discouraging the people of the Christian community from fighting about their religious beliefs. In Corinth he wrote letters to other Christian communities, including a letter to the Christian community in Rome.

In his letter to the Corinthians, Paul had promised to go to Corinth soon and help settle the questions that were bothering the Christian community. So he stopped there on his trip back to Jerusalem and stayed for a few months. Corinth had been a flourishing city of ancient Greece, but it was destroyed by the Romans in 146 B.C. Julius Caesar restored it around 44 B.C. Situated on the isthmus of Corinth, this city served as a port for shipping in the Ionian Sea and the Aegean Sea and thus enjoyed the wealth of a trading city.

The population of around 500,000 came from many places, hoping to earn great profits and live an easier life. But, of course, many people did not find wealth and success in the big city. They lived in poverty and worked at lowly jobs in the port. Paul preached among all classes of people and attracted many into the Church. There were disagreements and opposing groups within this church community. Paul worked to establish peace and harmony among his converts, who came from so many different backgrounds and therefore disagreed about many things.

When peace was restored, Paul collected some money to take to the community in Jerusalem, which was very poor. He also planned another missionary journey that would take him to Rome itself. There were already Christians in Rome, and so Paul wrote them a long letter. In this letter he talked a great deal about the importance of faith, telling the Romans that faith in Jesus Christ is the thing that saves us rather than human law or uprightness:

First, I thank my God through Jesus Christ for all of you, because your faith is proclaimed in all the world.... I long to see you, that I may impart to you some spiritual gift to strengthen you, that is, that we may be mutually encouraged by each other's faith.... [Romans 1:8-12]

Therefore, since we are justified by faith, we have peace with God through our Lord Jesus Christ. Through him we have obtained access to this grace in which we stand, and we rejoice in our hope of sharing the glory of God. [Romans 5:1-2]

Let love be genuine; hate what is evil, hold fast to what is good; love one another with brotherly affection; outdo one another in showing honor.... Rejoice in your hope, be patient in tribulation, be constant in prayer. Contribute to the needs of the saints, practice hospitality. Bless those who persecute you.... Rejoice with those who rejoice, weep with those who weep. Live in harmony with one another; do not be haughty, but associate with the lowly.... [Romans 12:9-16]

35. After returning to Jerusalem, Paul was arrested. He asked to be judged in Rome by the emperor because he was a Roman citizen. After many delays, the government transported him to Rome by sea and land. While awaiting trial, Paul preached and wrote, and after two years he was found not guilty. He then set out on another journey.

On his third missionary journey, Paul had collected some money for the Christian community in Jerusalem. When he arrived there, he met the leaders of the community and gave them the donations. One day in the temple, however, he was recognized by some Jews from the province of Asia, who stirred up the crowd against him (Acts 21:27). They had him arrested by the commander of the local Roman cohort of soldiers. Paul made it clear that he was a Roman citizen, which meant that he could not be punished until he had been legally condemned. He firmly insisted on being judged by the emperor in Rome.

After many delays (Acts 23-27), Paul was shipped off with other prisoners to Rome under the guard of a Roman centurion named Julius. Julius hoped to be in Rome by the beginning of October because it was unsafe to cross the sea as winter closed in. But they were still in Crete when October arrived. When they left Crete, the ship was battered by strong winds and heavy seas. The terrified passengers thought they were going to drown. Paul reassured them that there would be no loss of life. After fourteen nights at sea, they sighted a sandy beach at daylight and tried to run the ship aground on it. But the ship came apart on a sandbar, and everyone struggled to reach the shore.

Safely ashore on the island of Malta, they were treated well by the inhabitants during the winter. They set out for Italy in another ship when spring came. After several more stops, Paul finally arrived in Rome, where he was met by members of the Christian community. The government allowed him to take a lodging of his own, but a soldier was assigned to keep an eye on him. Meanwhile, Paul continued to proclaim the Gospel message, meet with visitors, and write letters. After two years, the government dismissed his case and set him free. He may have then visited Spain, as he had hoped to do, but it is also possible that his journey took him eastward instead. A second imprisonment in Rome later on would end with his martyrdom, which a very ancient tradition places in the year 67.

36. Although we have less information about Peter's missionary travels, tradition tells us that he eventually made his way to Rome and exercised his authority there as the head of the Christian community. He also kept in touch with other Christian communities, encouraging them in difficult times.

Christians had not been too badly treated by the Romans because they were regarded as a part of Judaism, a recognized religion in the Roman empire. Some Jews, though, saw Christianity as a false religion, and for that reason they tried in many ways to stop it from spreading. But the Roman government had not, at this time, passed laws against Christians.

The seeds of trouble were there, however. The humble lifestyle and virtuous living of the Christians probably aroused suspicion, scorn, and uneasiness amid the corruption and immorality of Rome. The Christians' refusal to worship idols and emperors may

At some point in his later years, Peter was in Rome, according to solid Church tradition. We have less information about him than we have about Paul, but it seems certain that he exercised supreme authority as the head of the Christian community in Rome and sought to give encouragement to its members. He also seems to have realized that more difficult times were coming for the Christian communities in various places, and that they needed encouragement in the faith.

Up to this point in time—the early 60s—

have raised suspicions of antigovernment activities. And the loving closeness of Christians to each other might well have aroused hostility and rumors of strange practices.

Peter wrote a letter to encourage Christians in their faith and to prepare them to meet their trials with courage and steadfastness. In it he urged them to remain faithful to the Gospel message and to their worldly tasks. If they wished to remain united with Jesus, they should stay in communion with the Church he had founded. Joy should be their attitude because they had once been lost sheep and now they were safely under Jesus' care. Even the need to make great sacrifices should not discourage them. As the letter put it (1 Peter 3:13-17):

> Now who is there to harm you if you are zealous for what is right? But even if you do suffer for righteousness' sake, you will be blessed. Have no fear of them, nor be troubled, but in your hearts reverence Christ as Lord. . . . keep your conscience clear, so that, when you are abused, those who revile your good behavior in Christ may be put to shame. For it is better to suffer for doing right, if that should be God's will, than for doing wrong.

37. Peter and Paul died as martyrs in Rome. Peter was condemned to be crucified, and he humbly asked to be crucified upside down. Paul, a Roman citizen, was beheaded. These deaths, according to tradition, happened during the persecution by Nero, following the great fire in Rome.

Peter's worries about possible persecution proved to be well founded when Nero became emperor at the age of sixteen. The full story of Nero is not clear, because the ancient reports about him came from Roman historians who were hostile to him. It seems fairly certain that Nero was a cruel ruler, who could not or would not use his power to help his people.

During Nero's reign, in the year 64, a terrible fire destroyed part of Rome. For six days and nights, the fire raged, burning some of the poorest sections of the city to the ground. Lost, too, were many beautiful old treasures and buildings that were important in Roman history.

Many people were homeless, hurt, or had lost their families and all their belongings.

Angry and frightened, they looked for someone to blame. Some people said that Nero had set the fire. There is reason to doubt this charge, but people did blame him as being responsible in one way or another. Some thought that the gods were punishing Rome for their emperor's wickedness. He had killed his own mother and his wife. The people began to say that the gods were angry with their emperor. Nero needed to turn the Romans' anger away from himself. He is probably responsible for blaming the Christians for the fire.

At that time, Christianity was a mysterious religion to the ordinary Roman citizen. Non-Christians did not understand the Christians' lifestyle. Romans could easily feel that Christians were to blame for the terrible fire.

And so the emperor's soldiers began to round up the Christians and cast them into prison. The government brought them before judges, who condemned them to cruel death for their crime of "hatred of the human race."

Peter was one of these victims. Sometime between the years 64 and 67, he was condemned to crucifixion. Tradition tells us that Peter did not feel worthy to be crucified in exactly the same way that Jesus had been killed, so he asked to be crucified upside down.

Tradition also tells us that Paul was imprisoned a second time in Rome during this period and condemned to death. But since he was a Roman citizen, he was beheaded rather than being crucified. The feast of Peter and Paul is celebrated on June 29.

38. In the year 66, Jews in Palestine began a revolt against the Romans and drove them out of Judea. But a large Roman army then attacked and took Jerusalem in the year 70. The city was sacked and burned, and the great temple was destroyed.

Judaism, which was under the protection of Roman law, had won many converts in areas outside Palestine. It was a widespread religion in the Roman empire. Between the years 66 and 70, however, it would suffer a devastating setback.

Judea, in southern Palestine, was occupied by the Romans and ruled by a Roman governor. The Jewish people, however, resented Roman rule and taxes. A party known as the Zealots preached armed revolt against the empire. They engaged in guerrilla attacks against the Romans. This kind of fighting was successful at first, and more followers joined the Zealot cause.

In the year 66, the Roman governor ordered his troops into the temple in Jerusalem

to haul off money and sacred vessels. This outrage caused the population to rise in revolt, and the Romans were driven from Judea. It seemed as if the Jews had regained their independence, but this would not last.

A large Roman army under the command of Vespasian, who would soon become emperor, gathered in Syria to march against Judea. Vespasian's son Titus accompanied him. In 67, the Roman army advanced into Judea. Many Jews took refuge in Jerusalem, where they stubbornly fought off the advancing Romans. Vespasian left for Rome upon becoming emperor, and Titus took command of the Roman army. In the year 70, Titus besieged Jerusalem. The inhabitants suffered terribly from lack of food, water, and supplies and from fighting among themselves. Titus took Jerusalem and ordered the city burned and the temple destroyed. Many rebel Jews were put to death, and others were enslaved or deported. The official sacrificial worship in the temple came to an end.

A later Jewish revolt that lasted from 131 to 135 led to the wiping out of Judaism in southern Palestine. For a while it seemed that the Roman empire might stamp out Judaism entirely. But with Roman approval, a new code of Jewish law, known as the Mishnah, was developed in Galilee. The Mishnah became the core of the Babylonian and Palestinian Talmuds and spread through the Greco-Roman world.

39. Spurred on by the teaching of Jesus and the course of events in the Church, some apostles probably scattered far and wide to preach the Gospel message. Church tradition tells us about Thomas and Andrew, for example, but we cannot be historically sure about their exact travels.

It seems quite likely that other apostles left Palestine and traveled around to preach the Gospel, just as Paul and Peter did. The Gospels tell us that Jesus told the apostles to go and preach to all nations. The growing Christian communities clearly felt that they had a mission to tell the world of Jesus.

Unfortunately, we do not have the same solid historical information about the travels of other apostles besides Peter, Paul, and John. But we will consider here what tradition has to say about the apostles Thomas and Andrew.

Tradition claims that Thomas went as far as India. We don't know if that is true, but such a trip was indeed possible using the caravan routes that stretched from Syria to India and beyond. Modern investigators

have been able to show that there was lively trade between Syria and India in the first century A.D., and that there may also have been a sea route between the two regions. In India, more than 1100 years later, explorers found hundreds of thousands of people who seemed to be following a form of Christianity, though India was not a Christian country. These people were called "Thomas Christians" because many people believed that they had descended from people who were taught by Thomas before the year 100!

Even today, there are many thousand "Thomasists" in India, and it is possible that these people trace their Christian heritage back to Thomas.

The apostle Andrew is supposed to have made his way by land and sea to a region in Europe then known as Scythia, which lies between the Danube River and the Dnieper River. This region would later be inhabited by the Slavic people we call Russians. Even today, the members of the Russian Church revere Andrew as the first one to bring the Gospel to their region.

Many Christians whose names we will never know helped spread the good news of Christ. As Christians traveled from place to place to go to markets or to visit friends and relatives, they must have talked to pagans they met about their religion. Pagans who were interested in Christianity probably gathered around their Christian friends to hear more about it. Some of these pagans would decide to be baptized. And so the Church grew stronger.

40. The disciple Mark is thought to have been a companion of Peter and to have written down Peter's memories of Jesus' life and teachings, forming the basis of the second Gospel in the New Testament. Mark is also supposed to have founded the Christian Church in Alexandria, Egypt.

The message of Jesus was proclaimed by other disciples besides the twelve apostles. One such disciple was the evangelist we know as Mark. After meeting Peter, Mark is reported to have traveled with him and to have written down Peter's memories of Jesus and his teaching. A reliable tradition says that these memories are contained in the Gospel according to Mark, the second Gospel in the New Testament.

We must realize, however, that the writing of the four Gospels was a complicated process that took place over a period of time. To say that Mark or some other evangelist was the author of a certain Gospel does not necessarily mean that he wrote the Gospel as we have it today. It is more likely that the Gospel in question came from a group of people or a community associated with the evangelist, and that the evangelist played some role in getting the story down in written form.

Mark is also supposed to have traveled to

Africa and established the Church in Alexandria. We cannot be sure about that, but we do know that Alexandria soon became a major center of Christianity. The city itself had been established by Alexander the Great in 331 B.C. It grew to become a major center of city life and serious thought in the Greco-Roman world. Jews went there in great numbers during the centuries just before the birth of Jesus. A famous and important translation of the Old Testament from Hebrew into Greek was done there by Jewish scholars. It is known as the Septuagint because it is supposed to have been done by seventy writers.

The Christian Church in Alexandria became a leading force in Christian life. And it is there that we find the first stirrings of the movement that would later be called *monasticism*. Some Christians left city life and worldly possessions behind to live alone or in small groups in the desert. There, far away from the distractions of the world, they could pray, think about God and his glorious works, and do penance for their sins and the sins of others. This way of life may have been inspired by certain Jewish and Indian practices, as well as by the example of Jesus. Later this movement would have a deep impact on the Western Church.

41. Around the year 90, all the apostles were dead except John. Living now in Ephesus, he continued to proclaim the teachings of Jesus. He told his followers that love for one another is the one great commandment.

By the year 90, all the apostles were dead except one. Only the apostle John was left alive, according to tradition, which claims that he was the youngest of the group.

John was with Peter in Jerusalem shortly after Pentecost, when Peter cured the crippled man in the temple. Apparently John was also in Jerusalem in the year 49 because Paul tells us he met him there. But tradition tells us that sometime later, perhaps during a period of persecution, John made his way to Ephesus. He may well have been accompanied by a community of Christian followers who regarded him as their leader. From the letters in the New Testament attributed to

him, it seems that John stressed the necessity of loving one's fellow Christians. He saw this as the one great commandment, and he preached this message to Christians in Ephesus and the surrounding area.

The fourth Gospel in the New Testament is also attributed to John. As we noted in the case of Mark, this does not mean that John necessarily wrote the Gospel as an author would write a book today. More likely, it means that the Gospel came from the teachings of John and from the Christian community gathered around him.

The fourth Gospel is noticeably different from the other three Gospels—Matthew, Mark, and Luke—which are called the Synoptic Gospels because they are so much alike. John's Gospel begins with the Word of God existing from all eternity and then coming down to dwell with human beings. It then presents a sovereign Jesus who always seems to be in complete control of what is happening, and who talks as though he and God are one and as though he himself will take the place of the Jewish religion. But there is also a tone of friendly closeness and love in his last talks to his own apostles. Long and serious thinking seems to have gone into the writing of this Gospel.

42. Toward the end of the first century, when many Christians were persecuted by the Roman emperors, a Christian writer named John recounted a series of visions that would form the final book in the New Testament. These visions consoled Christians during this period of persecution and assured them that the Church of Jesus would not be destroyed by its enemies.

After the persecution of Christians by Nero in the decade of the sixties, the Church was left in peace for some years. Then a later emperor named Domitian, who reigned from 81 to 96, created new difficulties for the Church. Seeking to restore stability to his sprawling empire, Domitian strictly enforced the laws that demanded allegiance to Rome and its emperor. Christians, who refused to worship the emperor as divine, were often forced to go into exile.

One such exile was the man who recounted the visions contained in the final book of the New Testament. He gave his name as John; but there are serious reasons for doubting that this man was the apostle John, although he may well have been associated in some way with the followers of that apostle. Living

in exile on the island of Patmos, not far from Ephesus, this John had a series of magnificent visions, which helped console Christians in this period of persecution. The visions assured Christians that the Church would not be destroyed by its enemies, because Jesus lived in victory with God, supporting his Church and preparing a reward for those who remained faithful to him.

The Book of Revelation—also known as the Apocalypse, which means *revelation* in Greek—is filled with symbols and vivid pictures. Such apocalyptic writings were fairly common in the Jewish world during the last couple of centuries before Jesus was born and for some time after. So the writer who called himself John was presenting a message that would not seem as strange to his audience then as it does to us today. But if we find out what the symbols mean, we too can understand the message.

At one point, for example, the writer described the persecution of a woman by a dragon and her eventual victory over the dragon (Revelation 12). It seems most likely that the woman symbolizes the people of God in the Old and New Testaments. The people of God in the Old Testament gave birth to the Messiah, who won victory over the forces of evil symbolized by the dragon. The people of Christ in the New Testament were thus ensured final victory over evil forces and persecutors. This is the message of hope and consolation that the author was trying to give his fellow Christians during a period of trials and sufferings.

43. In the year 112, Pliny the Younger, a ruler in one part of the Roman empire, asked the emperor Trajan whether he should hunt Christians down or wait until they were accused and then put them on trial. Trajan told him that if Christians were accused, they should be forced to give up Christianity and to worship the Roman gods. If they refused to do this, then they should be punished.

Part of the reason for this persecution was that the Romans, although they held many countries under their law, did not interfere with the details of the regional governments. This meant that the Romans did not try to protect Christians when they were persecuted. Another reason for the persecutions was the law passed by the emperor Nero stating that no one should be allowed to be a Christian. Because of this law, persecution could easily begin in places where the rulers or the people were against Christians.

We get some idea of the confusion and uncertainty surrounding the whole matter from a letter that Pliny the Younger, a

In the year 98, Trajan became emperor of Rome. Trajan is thought to have been one of the finest Roman emperors. He began relief programs for the poor, established homes for homeless children, and provided courts in which people who had been falsely convicted of crimes could have new trials. Yet Christians in the empire were persecuted.

regional ruler, sent to the emperor Trajan in the year 112. Pliny was the proconsul, or ruler, of Bithynia and Pontus. He had been arresting Christians, forcing some of them to give up their faith. He had killed those who remained loyal to their beliefs. Many people had been accused of being Christians. Some of them admitted it. Others claimed not to be Christians or said that they had been Christians but had given it up. Pliny asked Trajan what to do: Should he hunt these Christians down? There were many of them in his region—rich and poor, young and old, respectable citizens and more suspicious characters.

Trajan's reply was this: Do not hunt them out. If they are accused and admit that they are Christians, give them a chance to change their ways and worship Roman gods. If they will not worship in our way, they must be punished.

This reply was strange in some ways. After all, if Christians were doing something bad, they should be hunted down. But since the government said not to search for them, they apparently were not doing anything wicked. So why bother them at all?

Trajan's reply was unfortunate because later emperors were influenced by his views. His reply provided a basis for persecution.

44. By the beginning of the second century, the Roman empire was encountering several serious crises. Different peoples in the vast empire were revolting against Roman rule. Morality was at a low point, and the Romans were not sure what to believe in. Many different religions were attracting followers, and superstitious beliefs were spreading. Christians became scapegoats and were persecuted.

Pagan peoples and the Roman authorities now began to persecute Christians more frequently. This happened for a variety of reasons.

The situation in the Roman empire was worsening by the end of the first century. It was facing political, moral, and cultural crises. The very size of the empire was becoming a serious problem. It was so big that it was hard to defend its borders against outsiders and to keep all the subject people under control. When some people, such as the Jews for example, broke out in revolt, armies would have to be sent to put down the uprising. The Roman soldiers themselves were probably growing weary of warfare in distant lands and hoping to settle down to comfortable retirement in their native land.

The spread of the empire and increased communication also brought the Romans in contact with different cultures and religions. Many religions, particularly those in the East, were attractive to the Romans and cast doubts on the official religion of Rome. Some people no longer believed in any religion, and others clung to superstitious notions. The latter thought, for example, that a terrible fire meant that someone had committed a terrible sin or a crime. A lost battle meant that people had not prayed earnestly enough to Mars, the god of war.

This situation of doubt, uncertainty, and uneasiness was probably felt most by the common people, the masses, who were the first to suffer from economic, political, and social calamities. Thus there was every reason to look for some scapegoat on which to place the blame—such as those people known as Christians. The Christians refused to pray to the Roman gods or to honor the emperor. Their closeness to each other seemed somehow subversive, and their beliefs could be a dangerous example for would-be rebels. The people who wanted to unite and pull together the empire thought that something had to be done about these less-than-patriotic Christians. Yet, despite persecution from Romans, Jews, and pagan peoples, the number of Christians continued to grow.

45. As the first century drew to a close, a dispute broke out in the Christian community of Corinth. The people wanted to dismiss their bishop. Clement, the third bishop of Rome, intervened with a famous and important letter that settled the issue.

Leadership in the Church now passed to disciples of the apostles, since the apostles were all dead. These figures were called the Apostolic Fathers because they were close in time to the apostles themselves and did a great deal to preserve and pass on the Christian message handed down by the apostles.

One such Apostolic Father was Clement, the third bishop of Rome, who held that office from 92 to 101. Today we would say that he was the third pope, but we must remember that the term *papa* was used by many bishops at that time. It was only in the sixth century that it began to be applied solely to the bishop of Rome.

During the first few years of Clement's time as bishop of Rome, Christians there were persecuted by the emperor, Domitian. Bishop Clement must have helped his people with words of encouragement and prayer. And he probably kept informed of what was happening in churches outside Rome.

In the year 95, as the persecution was ending, Clement learned that there was a serious problem in the Christian community of Corinth. Many Christians in that city

refused to accept the authority of its bishop. They wanted to get rid of him and elect someone else in his place. Christian communities did have a role in choosing their leaders at that time, but this community already had a properly chosen bishop.

In the year 96 or so, Clement wrote a very important letter to the Christian community in Corinth. He wrote with an air of authority and made it clear that there was a hierarchy in the Church. The bishops were appointed by the apostles themselves, and other approved men were to succeed them in their office when they died. So the bishops received their office from Christ and God through the apostles. They had been entrusted with the mission of witnessing to the Christian truths taught by the apostles. The community needed to listen to its bishop and follow his directions in order to remain attached to the Christian message and to the authority of the apostles.

Clement's letter was favorably received by the people of Corinth and became an important precedent.

46. **Ignatius was the head of the Christian community in Antioch. This most famous and important of the Apostolic Fathers is remembered because of his letters.**

The Apostolic Father whom we remember most clearly is Ignatius, the bishop of Antioch. He was a link with the apostles because he was alive—as a young person—during the years that the apostles lived and preached.

Ignatius was taken to Rome in the year 110 and martyred. On his way to that city, he wrote seven important and moving letters. These letters have been saved, and we can still read them today. In them, we see a strong, brave man who was always ready to fight for faith and justice. His rule in life was, "In everything we do, remember always that God lives within us."

Ignatius's letters tell us that the local church communities were now in the process of being organized more strictly. One bishop was in charge, and he was helped by priests and deacons. The letters give a little picture of what was going on in his church around the time he was bishop.

There were already many Christians in the Church of Antioch, and new converts kept presenting themselves to be baptized and received into the community. Ignatius, like the apostles before him, sought out helpers. He laid his hands on certain persons and ordained them priests. They shared his work of helping the community and celebrated sacred services when he was absent or busy with other duties.

Like the apostles before him, Ignatius also ordained certain people as deacons. These deacons took charge of charitable works in the community and were of special help to the poor and the weak. Thus the Church of Antioch was solidly organized under the charge of one bishop.

The Christians in those early days, as they do today, obeyed Christ's words from the Last Supper and offered the Eucharist in memory of him. Celebrating the Eucharist was important in Antioch under Bishop Ignatius's leadership. Ignatius himself referred to Communion as the "medicine of immortality."

Ignatius preached to his people and urged them to remain faithful to Christ, following the Messiah's example and teaching his word. Jesus is the invisible bishop of every Christian community. The visible bishop must represent the community before Jesus, making sure that the community remains united with Jesus and faithful to his teachings. In this official task, the bishop has the help of the Holy Spirit.

47. Ignatius was denounced by pagans and condemned to death after a trial. He set out for Rome under guard. There his execution took place after a famous journey during which he offered inspiration and encouragement to many Christian communities.

The fame of Ignatius was widespread, not only in Antioch but in other parts of Asia Minor. He was known to the pagans, too. They saw him as a strong pillar of the Church, which they hoped to undermine by getting rid of Ignatius. He was denounced and, after a quick trial, condemned to death.

His judge decided that the execution of Ignatius should take place in Rome, so he was sent there guarded by two soldiers. The news spread quickly, and many Christians gathered to see and hear the brave bishop along his route to Rome. For all of them, he had words of consolation and encouragement. When Ignatius arrived in Smyrna, he

was met by Polycarp—another great figure of the early Church. The two friends and companions in the faith joined together in urging Christians to be faithful to Jesus and his love.

The situation of the Church was difficult because this was a time of persecution. But there was no reason to despair. Jesus would never abandon his faithful followers. Finding great joy and consolation in this thought, Ignatius decided to share it with other Christians. From Smyrna he wrote to several Christian communities, telling them that he was happy rather than sad about his coming death because he would soon be with Jesus. One of the letters was sent specifically to the Christians of Rome. Ignatius was the first to address the Church of Rome in a way that suggested Rome somehow presided over the bond of charity uniting all the local churches. What he meant exactly he did not say, and there has been much debate about it between Protestant and Catholic scholars.

Writing as if this were his last will and testament, Ignatius urged the Christians of Rome and their leader to watch over the faith of all the churches, and he paid them a moving tribute. He told the Christians of Rome not to be concerned about him and not to interfere with the Roman authorities on his behalf. It was wonderful, he wrote, to be "a setting sun on its way to God." He was afraid that their good will for him would do him harm by depriving him of this chance to meet God: "Even as grain must be ground up to make bread, so I desire to be sacrificed so that I may become a host pleasing to God."

From Smyrna Ignatius next went to Troas, where he wrote several more letters—one to his friend Polycarp. He finally was brought to Rome, where he was thrown to wild beasts. The example of this great-hearted bishop consoled many Christians, and he is remembered on February 1.

48. As Ignatius of Antioch and other leaders recommended, Christians worked to maintain unity within their individual communities and with Christian communities elsewhere. When Christian travelers arrived with news from other communities, they were probably welcomed joyfully, and their news was shared with the local community.

Christians had come to realize that love between the brothers and sisters of Jesus Christ was not easy. Sometimes envy and ambition created disharmony in their communities and raised the threat of harmful divisions. Disagreements and divisions existed from the very beginning because Christians were human beings. Later, these divisions would stand out even more clearly. But still, most Christians tried to stay united, to be attentive to each other's needs, and even to be concerned about other Chris-

At this point in the early second century, Christians in a given city or region began to belong to well-defined communities. Individual Christians belonged to a local church; church members knew each other and were under the leadership of a bishop.

Ignatius of Antioch had stressed the importance of unity among Christians. He had compared the Christian community to a choir in which all the members sang their praise of God in unison. Unity was important because

tians living far away. Letters and visits by missionaries helped the various communities to stay in touch with each other.

Christians traveling on a mission were well received by a community. But even some fellow Christian who happened to be traveling abroad on business probably got a friendly welcome. If he or she had a letter or some piece of news about a distant community, the exchange of information helped to strengthen the sense of relationship and brotherhood between the two communities.

A person who had never been seen before was not regarded as a total stranger if he or she were a Christian. That person shared the same faith and might have news to tell about his or her Christian community. People opened their doors and gave the stranger something to eat, hoping to hear the news and to share it with others. Together they could share the joys and sufferings of Christian communities in many different places and try to explore important questions about the Christian way of life.

49. We can imagine a traveling Christian bringing good news or bad news. He or she would cause excitement, and the local Christians would gather together to praise God for the continued existence of the Church amid trials.

A traveling Christian with news of some distant community would certainly be treated as an important figure by the local church community. Local Christians would want to meet the stranger, hear the news, and share experiences. Sometimes the news would be about martyrs and persecutions. Such news brought sadness, but it also proved the continuing growth of the Church amid trials.

We can readily picture a local community getting together to pray when it had heard such news. The visiting Christian would feel at home, even though the prayers and gestures of the local Christians might differ somewhat from those of his or her own Church. There was a basic similarity in the way that all Christians addressed themselves to God and prayed, particularly in the celebration of the Eucharist and in the saying of important prayers or readings. For all Christians everywhere sought to remain faithful to the heritage of the apostles, to what the apostles had handed down as the teachings and lessons of Jesus. They had the feeling of belonging to one and the same Church because they had worked hard to maintain unity.

Ignatius of Antioch had insisted that such unity must exist, and that it must be concrete and visible. He had said that the Christian community—the new people of God—was one single body. And he was the first to say that all the faithful everywhere made a *catholic*, that is, a universal, Church.

But the local church communities were not simply united in prayer and worship. The members were united in daily life and tried to help one another. They also tried to help distant communities, sending money or other aid when those communities needed it and when it was possible to do so.

50. Another great figure of the Church during the second century lived in Smyrna— Polycarp. As a young man, he had been a disciple of John the evangelist. Polycarp became bishop of Smyrna and the teacher of Irenaeus.

Asia Minor continued to be the place where the largest number of Christians dwelt and where the memory of the apostles was kept alive most vividly. The bishop of Smyrna, Polycarp, was one of the great witnesses to the apostolic tradition. We met him earlier when Ignatius of Antioch was on his way to execution in Rome.

Around the middle of the second century, there were few Christians left who had heard the message of Jesus directly from the lips of the apostles. One such Christian was Polycarp, who had been a disciple of the apostle John and who lovingly cherished the memory of this apostle and his message. We can imagine many Christians gathering around Polycarp to hear him tell about the life and teachings of John.

Polycarp had a particular affection for one of his young disciples named Irenaeus, who was around him constantly. He felt that Irenaeus would remember and cherish Polycarp's teaching, handing it down to other Christians. Polycarp would often call Irenaeus to him, telling him his most cherished memories, urging him to be faithful to the teachings of the Church, and stressing love for Jesus and for fellow Christians.

But as happened in the case of Ignatius of Antioch, the authority and influence of Polycarp in the local church came to the attention of pagans. Some of them decided to strike a blow at the Church by attacking the old bishop. They sought out Polycarp, captured him, and dragged him before the Roman magistrate. "This is the teacher of Asia, the father of the Christians, the destroyer of our gods, the one who teaches many people not to worship or sacrifice to our gods," they told the magistrate. "Strike a blow at him and the Christian Church will lose its vitality."

The magistrate questioned Polycarp and tried to convince him to sacrifice to the pagan gods. When Polycarp firmly refused, the magistrate condemned him to death. To increase his suffering, the magistrate ordered that he be burned alive at the stake. Polycarp remained unshaken. He undressed on his own and walked toward the stake, happy to give up his life for Jesus. Then he recited a solemn prayer, which gave courage and consolation to many Christians present:

> Father of your beloved and blessed Son Jesus Christ, through whom we have come to know you, the God of the angels, I praise you for considering me worthy to endure this day and this moment, to join the ranks of the martyrs and to share in the sacrifice of Jesus Christ. Be pleased to accept this sacrifice of mine, which I offer for your glory, that of Jesus Christ, your Son, and that of the Holy Spirit. Amen.

With this magnificent profession of faith, Polycarp died on February 22, 156.

51. In the year 177, many Christians in the city of Lyons were arrested and condemned to death. They had only to give up their faith and sacrifice to the emperor in order to save their lives. They chose instead to bear witness to Jesus and to accept death so that others would be led to believe in him.

Violent persecutions of Christians did not take place in Asia Minor only. One such persecution broke out in Lyons and Vienne, fortified towns in what is now southern France but what was then called Gaul.

In the year 177, a great festival in honor of the emperor was held in Lyons. People attended it from all parts of France. There were feasts and games, and a great sacrifice in honor of the emperor was held. The pagan participants became angry with the Christians for refusing to participate in any such sacrifice. Mobs attacked the homes of Christians and looted them. Pagans beat up Christians and dragged about fifty of them to the marketplace. There the Roman tribune questioned them briefly. When they confessed to being Christians, he had them put in jail.

During their trial the Christians were accused of not worshiping any god and of leading lives that brought misfortunes down on the town and the whole country. While these charges were being made, one Christian spectator pointed out that the Christians on trial had a right to be defended, and he offered to be their defender. Instead of honoring this re-

quest, the judge asked him if he was a Christian and had him arrested when he answered yes.

At this point some of the Christians on trial, seeing how harsh the judge was and realizing that they would be condemned to torture and death, were overcome with fear. Ten of them decided that they could pretend that they were not Christians, agree to offer the pagan sacrifice, and then return to the Church later. The remaining Christians were deeply saddened when the ten Christians told the judge that they did not acknowledge Christ. They all prayed earnestly to Jesus that these ten Christians might have strength and courage. Then they spoke to the weaker Christians: "Brothers, don't you realize that your behavior will harm the cause of Christ and the Church? The pagans are watching us. If we refuse to bear witness to our faith, even if it means death, how can we hope to convert pagans to Christ? Even other Christians will be discouraged by your example. And then, what about the salvation of your own souls and the reward that Jesus will give you if you are willing to die in honor of his name?"

These arguments helped to win back the weaker Christians, and all once again acknowledged their belief in Christ. The next day the entire group stood before the judge and praised the name of Jesus.

52. **Before being thrown to wild beasts, one of the Christians, Attalus, was paraded around the circus with a sign saying that he was a Christian. Although the sign was meant as a disgraceful insult, Attalus saw it as a mark of honor and joy.**

To no one's surprise, the trial of the Christians in Gaul ended with their condemnation to death. But they were not simply put to death. They were subjected to cruel treatment and torture. Some of them were burned to death; others were fed to wild beasts.

One case that makes a great impression on people is that of Attalus, a prominent and well-known Christian in Lyons. The pagans taunted him, saying that the governor would feed him to wild beasts on the big pagan feast-day when the crowd gathered for the circus games.

When the day came, Attalus was forced to parade around the amphitheater behind a big sign that read "Attalus is a Christian." The pagans thought that this would be a way to humiliate Attalus, but he was proud of what the sign said and walked around the grounds as one who had been given a great honor. Just as the crowd expected the wild beasts to be released, another Christian approached the governor and informed him that Attalus was a Roman citizen. Reluctantly, the governor

had to send Attalus back to jail so that he could be tried again as a Roman citizen.

Present at the new trial was a Christian doctor named Alexander. While Attalus and the other Christians on trial were being questioned by the judge, Alexander kept urging them to remain firm in their faith. He also kept helping them with answers to the judge's questions. Finally, the angry judge called Alexander and asked him who he was. "A Christian," replied Alexander. The judge had him arrested immediately.

The second trial ended with death sentences too. Both Alexander and Attalus were tortured and fed to wild beasts while a crowd watched.

How different was the behavior of the Roman authorities from that of the Christians! The authorities wanted to kill all the Christians, to rid their territory of them. And yet they did not really seem to have any good reason for doing so. It was just that the Christians did not live the same way as they did and did not offer sacrifices to the emperor. Meanwhile, the Christians bravely and serenely endured suffering and death because they felt united with Jesus and strengthened by his support.

53.
Now learned pagans began to attack Christianity also. Fronto, the tutor of emperor Marcus Aurelius, attacked Christianity in a speech before the Roman senate.

Lucian, a satirist, ridiculed Christians in his writings. Celsus, a serious thinker, studied Christianity carefully but found its teachings unacceptable.

As we noted earlier, opposition to Christianity was first evident among certain Jews and pagans for a variety of reasons. To Jews, the new faith seemed to be a Jewish heresy— a falling away from the true Jewish religion and an act of religious disloyalty. Some pagans thought Christianity threatened their commercial interests or their traditional way of doing things. And some Roman authorities thought Christianity seemed like rebellion.

It was not until the second half of the second century that Roman thinkers and writers began to attack Christianity or to make fun of it in writing. Such attacks indicated that the new faith was growing more important in society. The attacks also posed a new danger for the Church. Anti-Christian hatred and prejudice, when put down in clever written form, appealed to a wide public. These writings influenced many non-Christians who until now had not approved of persecuting Christians.

The first educated pagan to speak out against the lifestyle and teachings of Christians was Fronto. He was the tutor of a future emperor, Marcus Aurelius, and so he was very influential. Asked by the Roman senate to give his opinion of the Christians, Fronto made a long speech in which he supported various prejudices against Christians. He said that the Christians' way of life was worthy of condemnation in every respect. At their gatherings they ate and drank too much, got drunk, and did all sorts of terrible or obscene things. Their teachings were foolish, not worthy of serious consideration or study.

Lucian of Samosata attacked Christianity in a different way. He was a writer of satire, poking fun at people and ideas by making them sound ridiculous and concentrating on the funny side. This is what he did when he wrote about Christians or their beliefs. He made fun of their way of living and praying. He made them seem like naive people who could be easily deceived.

A third anti-Christian was Celsus. He was a serious thinker, and he did not take Christianity lightly. A lover of Greek learning, he wanted to know more about the Christian way of life and Christian beliefs. He discussed these things with Christians and read some of their writings—the Gospels in particular. After devoting some time to this study, he wrote a learned work that became very popular with Roman readers. In it he came to the conclusion that he could not accept Christian teachings because they were not in agreement with the culture and thinking of learned persons—and of learned Greeks in particular. For one thing, Celsus could not believe that God, out of love, would come to earth to save human beings.

54. Some learned pagans converted to Christianity and became strong defenders of the faith. One such person was Justin, who was a student of philosophy in his youth. After he became a Christian, he made his way to Rome, where he founded a school. He taught the truths of Christianity, defended them against pagan attacks, and tried to show how Christianity could be reconciled with the thinking of the great pagan philosophers.

Not all challenges are fatal. In the face of accusations and attacks from pagan writers, Christians were forced to defend their beliefs and think about them more deeply. This helped Christians to understand their faith better, and it helped pagans to get a clearer picture of how Christians thought and lived their lives.

A speech defending one's point of view was known as an *apologia* in Greek. That is where we get our word *apology* in English, but the meaning has changed a great deal since the second century. Then an apology was a defense of one's way of thinking or acting, and so we talk about a group of men known as the Christian apologists. One such man was Justin the Martyr, who is regarded as the most important of the Christian apologists. But this does not mean that he was a great writer or that his presentation of Christian belief was completely sound and clear. He was more like a trail blazer, a pioneer in serious Christian thinking.

Justin was born into a Greek family living in Palestine. His family sent him to the best teachers of the day for his schooling. Justin had an open mind and was sincere in his search for truth. He was not completely satisfied with what he learned, and he was not convinced by all the accusations against Christians.

One day, it seems, Justin met an old man by a river bank. The two started talking, and the old man told Justin that it was the prophets of the Old Testament and Jesus Christ who had uncovered the truth—not the pagan thinkers. Justin thought this over for some time, and eventually he became a Christian. After traveling around to proclaim and teach the Christian faith, Justin settled in Rome and opened a school of Christian philosophy.

In the year 150 he wrote a famous defense, an apology, of the Christian faith and sent it to the emperor, Antoninus Pius. In it he defended Christianity against the charges of atheism and political rebellion that had been made against it. His other writings, like many of the writings of Christians and others in these centuries, have not survived. But we do possess his *Dialogue*, which offers a defense of the Christian viewpoint according to the writings of the Old Testament.

Justin and some of his followers were martyred in the year 165, under the reign of Marcus Aurelius.

55. Some Christians adopted views and ways of living that did not agree with the teachings of the apostles. Some sought to keep Christianity more closely tied to the Mosaic law and Jewish practices. Some claimed to have a special

kind of knowledge that only few could attain. And others combined various ideas into their own particular kind of religion. Marcion was a man who made his own religion by distorting Christianity.

There were threats to the teachings of Jesus and the apostles from inside Christianity also. From the very beginning, it seems that some groups of converted Jews tried to keep Christians bound to the Mosaic law and older Jewish practices. Even when the Church had become clearly aware of its separation from Judaism, groups known as Judaizers continued to insist that Christians follow all the practices of the Jewish religion.

Another threat came from people who claimed to have a higher kind of knowledge, a *gnosis,* which was handed down secretly and known only to a few. This viewpoint had taken shape before the birth of Jesus through a mixture of ideas from Eastern religions and Greco-Roman thought. Around the year 150, it began to pose a strong challenge to the true Christian view of God and the world. Seeing the material world as evil, gnosticism taught that salvation came through being free from matter. Jesus was seen as a higher being, not truly human, who revealed a new and unknown God to human beings. The Gnostics thought that their new, secret knowledge could be used to reach the fullness of light and perfection apart from matter.

A third threat came from people who combined various ideas from different sources to formulate their own version of Christianity. One major figure of this sort was a man named Marcion, who was born at Sinope in Pontus around A.D. 85. His father, a bishop, eventually banned him from the local Christian Church for wrong ideas and practices. Marcion became a wealthy shipowner and went to Rome somewhere around the year 139. He joined the Christian Church there and generously donated his funds to it. But about five years later, he began to propose his own ideas and separated from the Church. Gathering followers, he organized his own church with its own bishops and priests. Its members were often devout and zealous people, and some of them suffered martyrdom. The Marcionite Church spread fairly widely and rapidly, and it continued to exist in some form even after its views had been officially rejected by the Christian Church.

According to Marcion, the creator God of the Old Testament was not the redeemer God of the New Testament. The creator God was a vicious, angry being, and the Jewish religion was to be rejected and despised completely. Only the loving God revealed by Jesus—who only seemed to have taken on a human body and who was completely hostile to the Jewish law—was to be obeyed and worshiped. Marcion was very interested in the concrete practice of religion, but here again he set up strict demands that went too far. The full-fledged members of his religion were obliged to give up marriage, for example, and material things were regarded as suspect, if not totally evil.

In the fight against such extreme views, the Christian Church was required to strengthen its own form of organization and to spell out its teachings more clearly.

56. Irenaeus, the disciple of Polycarp, made his way to Lyons when he grew up. Becoming the bishop there, he wrote important doctrinal works, participated actively in disputes, and did missionary work among the Celtic people in Gaul. Though many of his writings have not survived, he is regarded as the most important theologian of the second century.

want to know what correct Christian doctrine and living are, said Irenaeus, we must consider what the Church has taught and lived from the beginning up to our own day.

Irenaeus went to Rome to take part in the discussion about erroneous views. In Rome, a Christian named Montanus preached a very strict kind of Christianity. The Roman Church decided at this time not to condemn these views. Later on, it would become plain that the Montanists were not simply overly enthusiastic Christians but holders of mis-

Irenaeus, the young disciple of Polycarp, moved from Smyrna in Asia Minor to Lyons in Gaul when he grew up. He first served as a priest under the bishop of that region, Pothinus, and then took the place of this bishop when Pothinus was martyred.

Irenaeus was a very intelligent person. He used his abilities to defend the faith against mistaken ideas and practices that were now spreading through the various Christian communities. Irenaeus gave a detailed defense of tradition and Church authority. If we

taken views, and Montanism would be rejected by the Church.

In Lyons, Irenaeus was very active as a missionary bishop. Places such as Lyons, which were called towns or cities at the time, were really little more than the headquarters for the local Roman authorities and their troops. Most of the local population lived in the surrounding countryside. In the time of Irenaeus, many of these local inhabitants were pagan Celts, and Irenaeus worked earnestly among them.

Irenaeus also tried to answer the questions that were being debated in his day. What about sins committed after Baptism? Some Christians of his day felt that Baptism gave Christians a special gift, and that they should not commit any sins after Baptism; if they did, they could not be saved. Irenaeus made it clear that God is willing to grant salvation to any and all sinners who do penance for their sins. Because of his work and his writings, Irenaeus is regarded as the most important theologian of the second century.

57. By the end of the second century, the Christian Church had decided which writings truly mirrored the teachings of Jesus and the apostles. As a defense against erroneous views and writings, these writings were gathered together to form the New Testament. The Christian Church also accepted the Old Testament as a proper part of its Bible.

By the end of the second century, the Church of Jesus had reached an important stage in its growth. It had come through persecutions, and it had faced up to the threat of outside attacks and erroneous teachings by some Christians. It seemed advisable, perhaps even necessary, to decide which Christian writings truly reflected the teaching of Jesus and his apostles and to gather these writings together as a sound body of Christian thought. For this reason, the Church formed the canon, or the official list, of writings that now make up the New Testament. The formation of the canon took place over a period of many years, and the New Testament as we know it was fairly well established by the year 200. The Church also determined that the whole Old Testament should be a part of the Bible of the Christian Church. These writings can be found in the Bible today.

Let us briefly review the process that led to the formation of the Christian Bible. First of all, the apostles had followed Jesus' instructions to preach the good news he had announced. They went from place to place proclaiming his message, talking about his life and deeds, and founding communities that would live by his message.

At some point after Jesus' departure from this world, people began to put this message, and other memories of Jesus, into written form. This was a gradual, complicated process. With the help of the Holy Spirit, certain Christian individuals and groups helped to develop the writings that make up the four Gospels and the other books of the New Testament. The introductions in many good modern translations of the New Testament explain this whole process.

After the apostles died, the leaders of Christian communities who had known the apostles and been taught by them became important witnesses to the message of Jesus as handed down by the apostles. Thus, besides the writings that would later be collected in the New Testament, the Church had the spoken recollection of Christian leaders from age to age. This body of spoken teaching and memories is known as tradition, that is, something handed down.

When the Church was faced with problems or incorrect views, it would turn to its written record in the Bible (also known as Scripture) and to the tradition it had received from earlier Christian witnesses and authorities. The Church would continue to think about its heritage, to develop Christian ideas further, and to apply them to new situations and problems. But the body of teachings derived from Jesus and the apostles would remain the deciding standard behind all future developments.

58. By the year 180, there were many Christians scattered far and wide. They were most numerous in the eastern Mediterranean and in Asia Minor. The Church was becoming very large.

The Christian faith had now spread far and wide around the eastern shores of the Mediterranean Sea. It was also making its way deeper into regions farther away from the sea.

In Palestine itself, the Christian community had consistently faced problems from zealous Jews. After the destruction of Jerusalem, the Church had recovered somewhat, but it faced new persecution when a false Messiah named Bar Kosiba led a revolution against Rome in the second century. After the defeat of this uprising, the Christian communities in Palestine were made up of converted Greek-speaking peoples and Romans.

Christianity continued to grow in the various cities of the empire. Antioch remained a great Christian center, cherishing the testimony and example of Bishop Ignatius. From Antioch, Christian missionaries set out for cities and rural areas farther east, traveling to Mesopotamia and perhaps even India. There were also Christian communities in northern Arabia and in Egypt. Alexandria was an important center of Christianity, and in 190, it was guided by Bishop Demetrius.

Christianity also flourished along the coast of Asia Minor and in the interior. Small groups of Christians existed among the rural population, and the Church of Ephesus held a special place in the eyes of Christians because of its Christian traditions going back to Paul.

In Greece, Corinth was emerging as a major center of Christianity because of its intense religious life and the great ability of the bishops in charge of its Church. In Italy, the big center of Christianity was Rome. Its Christian population was made up of people